Bilbo the lifeguard dog

Steven Jamieson was born in the Shetland Islands.
He briefly worked for the Ministry of Defence before
adopting a life of freedom as a waterman and lifeguard
in, on and by the sea at Land's End, Cornwall.

D1424455

Bilbo

the lifeguard dog

A true story of friendship and heroism

STEVEN JAMIESON

with ALISON BOWYER

PAN BOOKS

First published 2016 by Sidgwick & Jackson

First published in paperback 2017 by Pan Books
an imprint of Pan Macmillan
20 New Wharf Road, London N1 9RR
Associated companies throughout the world
www.panmacmillan.com

ISBN 978-1-5098-2141-9

1 3 5 7 9 8 6 4 2

A CIP catalogue record for this book is available from the British Library.

Typeset by Ellipsis Digital Limited, Glasgow
Printed and bound by CPI Group (UK) Ltd, Croydon, CR0 4YY

To the memory of Bilbo the lifeguard dog,
my best friend and saviour,
and the Legendary Penwith Lifeguards
1971–2008

Preface

Gwynver beach in the far west of Cornwall is one of those places where, on a good day, you could be anywhere in the world. It's paradise. It holds its own with the best Caribbean beaches and the heat that can be generated in the summer months is surprising. The hottest part of the day can often be around five o'clock but you can stay down there until half ten just in your shorts. On a warm, still summer's night, myriads of glow-worms on the cliff light up the footpaths and the water glitters with magical phosphorescence, turning the waves luminous green. The phosphorescence only appears at certain times of the year, when the algae bloom comes in, and you have to be really lucky to see it. Some nights, with a full moon shining on pristine white sand, you could even imagine it as a snowy scene with the rocks showing up jet black in the silvery moonlight.

And that was my office. Sometimes I wouldn't bother to go home at all and would kip on the beach, listening to the crickets and the crackle and spit of a driftwood fire with the sound of the waves breaking on the shore. You can forget your corporate penthouses on top of skyscrapers, the view from my place of work – of Land's End and the great Atlantic Ocean – was the best in the world. Even the commute was great. I'd just open the door of my bijou home, which was actually three sheds knocked together and painted black, and wander down the cliff path to the sea.

I was a lifeguard and that was my calling for over thirty years. I lived and breathed it and, to be honest, I didn't want anything more from life. I lived simply, in said hut, which was basic to say the least, but what could you expect for thirty quid a week? I called it Chez Noir. During the winter when storms would batter the cliffs around Land's End, I would often lie in bed at night and listen to the wind blowing. There was one thick beam running the length of the ceiling, and I remember lying there one night when it was particularly windy and watching the beam move up and down about ten centimetres as the wind tried to suck the roof off. The next morning I got up and tried my utmost to move that beam and I couldn't.

It was so quiet; there were no car or house alarms to disturb the morning's peace until the first Land's End aeroplane to the Isles of Scilly took off at ten to eight. The planes would fly right over my shed and because it didn't have any insulation, it felt like I was lying outside. Other than that the only plane noise was the sonic boom from Concorde when it used to fly over twice a day.

Chez Noir had no facilities to speak of and in winter months I used to have to wear my clothes in bed to keep warm: tights, tracksuit bottoms, fleece hat, double duvet – the works. I lived like that for ten years and did nothing to the place at all, then one day I suddenly thought: This is ridiculous! And I asked a friend of mine to make me some

French doors, cut a hole in the shed, stick the doors in and build a veranda out the front. At the same time I insulated Chez Noir.

You could have sat out there completely rawhide if you wanted to and it wouldn't have mattered. Nobody could see you from anywhere around. No footpaths overlooked me, and all you looked out on was the sea, with the sun going down. Sometimes, if you were especially lucky, you could witness the 'green flash'. As the sun sinks below the horizon, if conditions are right, for an instant a green light glows just at the point of sunset. Green, like the aurora borealis. On a fine day you could even see the beaches on the Isles of Scilly.

My mate Lloyd used to call my life the golden triangle: beach, pub, home. I think he envied me. Hell, I envied me. It was a great life and to my mind it couldn't get better.

How was I to know that in fact there was a huge, bear-sized gap in my existence, just waiting to be filled . . .

1

Once a Waterman . . .

I feel privileged to be a waterman: someone who makes their living from the ocean and understands the weather and the tides and the sea. It's not just a matter of being a lifeguard or a fisherman, or a good surfer – it's more all-encompassing than that, rather it is about knowing everything to do with the sea.

Having practically been brought up on a boat, it was second nature to me really. I was born at the opposite furthest-flung end of the UK, on the Shetland Islands. My eldest daughter Alice says the reason I live the way I do – favouring a spartan existence with few material possessions – is because I'm from Shetland, and she's probably right. It was a hard life and Shetlanders didn't live much beyond forty back in the day. All my family were born on Shetland and we can trace our ancestry to an area in Norway, north of Bergen. The Vikings sailed across to Shetland from Norway and to this day Shetland boats are based on long-ships and are double-ended like the Vikings' boats.

I was born in 1951 in Lerwick, which is the main port in the Shetland Islands, in an old army Nissen hut because there wasn't a proper maternity hospital on the islands at the time. My mum's name was Nell Reid and she was a beauty who dreamt of being an airline stewardess. My dad, James Cameron Bowie Jamieson, was a GPO engineer. He started out as a tea boy and worked his way up to become a technician installing telephones to the islands in Shetland. There were no ferries to those islands, just a small boat. I went with him once or twice, not very often though because it wasn't always possible for him to make it home the same day. In the winter the boats quite often couldn't get back because the sea was so rough and Dad would have to stay wherever he was working. Sometimes he was away for three or four weeks at a time.

It was hard in those days because things were a bit more primitive. Apart from basic hospital treatment or A&E, if you needed anything more specialized you had to go to Aberdeen, and the only way to get there was by boat or fixed-wing aircraft. The St Clair ferry sailed between Shetland and Aberdeen but quite often it wouldn't be able to make the crossing because the sea was so rough. So if something happened to you in Shetland and the weather was bad, well, it was tough luck – you just had to wait.

I was my parents' firstborn and was really close to them. They were very kind people who had to endure great heartache in their lives. I grew up knowing that I'd had two sisters who died, both while very young. Years later, after both my parents had passed away, I discovered there was quite likely a third sibling who also died.

The first sister who passed away died of complications at birth, at least from what I can gather; Mum wouldn't talk about it. I would have been about five at the time. Her name was Susan. She never came home as far as I can remember. Something happened and she died, though I think she went full-term. I'm not sure what it was that happened because Dad never talked about it either.

My second sister, Lynne, died five years later when I was about ten. She was only about eighteen months old. I asked Mum about it again shortly before she died. That morning I had put my finger in Lynne's mouth for her to suck on to stop her screaming. And Mum had said, 'Never put your fingers in the baby's mouth because they're dirty.' So I thought I'd made her ill and I went and hid under the stairs and wouldn't come out. Later, I pleaded with her, 'Mum, please tell me what happened.' But she wouldn't. I think it was meningitis because I remember Lynne scream- ing and screaming. The nurse came to the house and said, 'This baby has to go to hospital immediately.'

They needed to take Lynne to Aberdeen but no aero- planes were flying because the weather was so bad and there was thick fog. By a day or so later when it was clear enough to fly the disease must have progressed too far. And that was the last time I ever saw my baby sister. I remember my dad coming up the stairs one morning. I was in bed with my mother, and I'll never forget it because he walked up those stairs as if he had lead in his shoes. I could hear the thud of them on each step: *thump, thump, thump.* And he came in and just said: 'She's gone, Nell.'

Mum and Dad didn't say a word to me about my sister dying. In fact, they were so protective and secretive about it that shortly afterwards they told me not to go to school my normal way. I was to go via a muddy park, a route I never usually used. When Mum said, 'Why don't you go through the park to school this afternoon?' I couldn't understand why and said, 'Yeah, yeah,' but I didn't go that way – I went the usual route with all my mates. Halfway there, I met the funeral cortège coming round the corner, with the coffin and my grieving dad (the womenfolk in Shetland rarely, if ever, went to a funeral service or burial in those days).

I couldn't understand why I wasn't included in Lynne's funeral. I can see now that they were trying to protect me, of course. Back then, in my family at least, things weren't discussed. And it affected me in strange ways. Suddenly, at eleven years old, I started wetting the bed and I developed a speech impediment that I would struggle with in the coming years.

I think Lynne's passing destroyed my parents too. To lose those children must have been grim. It was the sixties, and it wasn't par for the course. My dad contracted Parkinson's disease soon after Lynne died. And some said it was the shock of her dying which was to blame. All I know is that after that he got really ill and he never recovered. He was about thirty-five when he contracted it and he died when he was fifty-nine. My mum single-handedly cared for him for twenty years.

Growing up in Shetland was as quiet and idyllic a childhood as you might expect. Life there is completely intertwined with the sea. There weren't many roads up until the late 1800s so before they started putting tarmacadam down and building roads everybody travelled by boat. Although it's only sixty miles long there's something like a thousand miles of coastline in Shetland because it's all fjords and inlets. My village of Walls is at the head of a protected and very sheltered bay. My friends and I had our own rowing boats, and the many small islands within the bay were ideal playgrounds for us. We would be explorers or pirates, or would visit deserted beaches and skim stones.

I taught myself to swim when I was eleven. There were no swimming pools in Shetland and the water wasn't particularly warm, but it was relatively safe. Despite that, I remember having to rescue a friend of mine, a boy called Ronnie, even though I'd only just learnt to swim at the time. In Shetland we have this long seaweed that comes up like bootlaces from the bottom and hangs in the water. Ronnie got into a patch of this weed and panicked, and when you start thrashing and floundering around the seaweed kind of grabs hold of you. He was only about six metres off the shore and the sea wasn't that deep, but he was in trouble and started shouting for help.

We were the only ones there and I swam out and managed to get hold of him and dragged him back in to the shore. It was just a matter of hanging on to him and pulling him away from the weeds. It wasn't a big deal at the time – I don't think either of us even told our parents. So that was the first time I rescued anybody – little did I know I was to have a career in lifesaving.

My grandfather, a Shetland JP, ran the local shop and my aunt was the postmistress. They also kept sheep, and it was my grandfather who taught me everything about them: how to look after them, how to shear them, dispatch them and butcher them. From that I got an understanding of all animals. They weren't just things that stood there; they were living creatures and they had feelings. And they've all got feelings, even fish – I don't care what anyone says. The mistreatment of animals is one thing that'll always stir up strong emotions in me.

If there are a few people in the room and there's an animal, normally the animal will come and sit with me – a definite drawback with Customs dogs! I've always been good with them, had a way with them if you like. To this day, if there's an animal around I'll befriend it, whether it's a sheep in a field or somebody's cat.

I used to try and creep up on sheep and rabbits when I was a kid, just for something to do. I would go out into the hills and pretend I was a Red Indian and try and catch a rabbit. You could catch a sheep if you were really quiet and stealthy and slowly crept, but I was never able to catch a rabbit. I also used to do what the Scottish call 'guddling' trout, where you tickle the underbelly of the fish that were often hanging about under the bank of streams. The fish would go limp and I'd scoop them out of the water with my hands.

We had a dog, a little white and brown terrier with wiry hair, but he never spent much time with me. He was always Dad's dog. I don't remember him going anywhere with me; he just hung around at home. I must have been about twelve when he came, because it was only a year or so after my sister Lynne died. He had been caught chasing sheep out in the countryside and his owners asked Dad if he wanted him. They were going to put him down otherwise, so Dad brought him home. The dog, unbelievably, was called Linn. Of course Mum and Dad didn't want the reminder of Lynne's name every day so they changed his name to Kim. He went on for years and lived to be about fifteen.

I was nineteen when I left Shetland to work on a successful stud farm in Worcestershire as a stable lad for a few months. There were quite a few dogs knocking around the stables but I never took much notice of them. It was the horses I was interested in; I wasn't really attracted to dogs at all in those days. Strange, when you think how my life would later be turned upside down by one.

But that was all in the future.

2

Surf's Up

Funny, really, that I should go from living at one end of the country to the other. But because I was from Shetland, Land's End held an enchanting appeal for me and when I eventually got here I found the people to be very similar to Shetlanders.

In 1972 I was doing a DJ spot in Penzance at the local venue for bands, The Winter Gardens, or 'Wints' as it was known locally. Some amazing bands appeared there before they became famous – groups such as AC/DC, 10cc, The Sex Pistols and Lemmy, pre Motorhead days. I ran the first mobile stereo disco in west Cornwall and named my set-up Shadowfax, playing records before the bands came on.

I would normally set up my kit in a corner of the stage, but on this particular night the heavy metal band Judas Priest was performing and they refused point blank to share the stage at all. 'Get all this off the stage!' they said, pointing at my turntables. 'We don't want any of this *stuff* here, it's all got to go down onto the dance floor.' Well, I stormed off up to the restaurant and sat down to cool off. I already knew some of the staff at Wints and it was there, whilst having a coffee, that I met a young girl who would go on to become my wife. Sadly, we weren't destined to stay together, but we remain friends and enjoy watching our three children grow and flourish.

When I first moved to Cornwall I couldn't believe how different the sea was from Shetland. The main difference is the swell (waves which are generated by depressions in the Atlantic blowing winds over the sea). The Shetland Islands rise steeply out of the ocean and almost no swell waves reach Shetland's sheltered beaches, whereas around Land's End massive swells created in the Atlantic hit far more exposed beaches. Every now and again we see a pulse of swell waves which we call 'sets'. Some sets have only three to four waves and arrive every fifteen minutes while others can arrive every five minutes and contain ten waves in each set. So you can have a group of waves arriving that are quite big, then you'll get a period of anything up to twenty minutes when the waves are relatively small, and then another group of big waves come in. That's what all surfers wait for.

A lot of people who come to the beach don't understand that all waves are not equal. If you've got a big ground sea, which is a swell that's come a long way – say from the eastern seaboard of the United States where a big hurricane's blown up – it will have generated swell all the way across the Atlantic. A wind swell, on the other hand, is a locally produced swell with not much fetch – or distance – behind it, so has much less power. Charts help determine where the swell's going to hit, so an experienced surfer will be able to look at a weather chart and think: Right, there's going to be swell here on that day. It's crucial to guess correctly just when it would first arrive so as to have those first waves to yourself.

When I first moved to Cornwall I got a job at the Ministry of Defence, on the outskirts of Camborne, working for the research side of the RAF Met Office. We had access to the latest synoptic pressure charts and time charts. After work I would rush down to the beach to the lads and say, 'Look, there's a big swell that's being kicked up here!' I became quite valuable to the surfers. They'd say, 'When's the swell coming, J'mo?' (that's my nickname, pronounced Jaimo) and I'd say, 'I'll get you a chart.' I suppose that's when I began my education as a waterman.

Once I discovered the surfer's way of life, it became harder and harder to be stuck behind a desk from nine to five. Eventually, I couldn't take it anymore; I handed my notice in and said, 'I'm out of here – I'm going to the beach to work.' I spent a spell at SkewJack Surf Village in Porthcurno, the first surf school in the UK, as a part-time lifeguard and a DJ by night. The Village was an old RAF camp and Mr T, the handyman, was never short of work. It was full of wooden billets and the bar had a sprung wooden dance floor, making it an ideal off-the-wall holiday club for young people. The mid to late seventies was a magical time and I happened to slot into it. Everyone was in full party mode. There were no helmets on motorbikes and no drink-driving laws. We had car crashes and goodness knows what else. The lanes in Cornwall tend to have right-angle corners and quite often the cars would go straight on through the hedgerow and into the field, and so 'Skewjack corner' became legendary. Luckily there was not much in the way of traffic in those days.

In 1978, I started working for Penwith District Council as a lifeguard on the beach at Sennen Cove and fell in love with it. Sennen, and in particular Gwynver, probably has the most consistent surf in the UK and when I started I was thrown in at the deep end with these guys called the Bryant brothers. Jonny and Nick Bryant were rugby players, surfers and general hell-raisers who weren't too keen on people who were different to them. I had fairly long hair at the time and was just getting into the surfing culture, so they were immediately suspicious of me. I felt their attitude was: 'Who's this guy who's done one year at SkewJack Surf Village and thinks he's going to work on the beach with us?'

Penwith District Council's lifeguard service was in its infancy and it was the first time we'd worked as a team on Sennen, although the Bryant brothers had already had at least one season's lifeguarding experience and were more competent surfers than me. However, we became really good mates and that's when I realized that it's all to do with the team, and that it doesn't stop at six o'clock either. If we went out for the evening and anything kicked off we were all going to look after one another. We would get a lot of people who would challenge us. It's different now because lifeguarding has become the norm. They also have help now from Police Community Support Officers, who can come down and back them up when things get really rough. But in those days people would threaten you in the car park after work. They'd say, 'We'll be waiting for you in the car park, big mouth.' We'd walk across the beach thinking: If they're there, we're all in this together, lads. Luckily, it didn't kick off very often.

In the early days before we had radios, we had to rely

on whistling and hand signals to communicate with one another. We were the first team of lifeguards to work on Sennen. Prior to that, the local authority pre-Penwith Council provided lifeguard cover on selected beaches deemed to be 'at risk'. It was pretty basic, with the lifeguard – usually a surfer or travelling Aussie – being given a rescue board, a rescue torpedo or 'can', a pair of binoculars, and instructions to 'Carry on'. Wages would be paid into his account weekly but there was no formal contract. It was more a case of: 'See you at the end of the season.'

Jeff Devaney and Keith Miller were the first in a new line of lifeguards working for the newly formed Penwith District Council in 1974. Jeff lived for the summer months in a caravan behind the toilets in Sennen car park with his long-suffering partner (being the girlfriend of a surfer is akin to being a golf widow), and was one of a line of legendary guys who came back year after year to work the beaches around Land's End.

It was in the leaky old lifeguard hut, high on the dunes, that Nick, Jonny and I used to sit on drizzly summer days, taking the mickey out of one another and estimating how much money the cafe and car park owner would make over the holiday period. We had a right laugh, and thank goodness we did, because amongst all those hours of hilarity we formulated what would become known as an EAP, or Emergency Action Plan. Although we did not realize it at the time, all the scenarios we discussed idly were about to prove extremely useful. We relied on each of us being completely 'in tune'; we were, in effect, pioneering a new way of working as a team. And on 14 August 1979, the same day as the infamous Fastnet disaster when lots of boats capsized, we were called into action for what is still possibly one of the most successful genuine mass rescues carried out by beach lifeguards in the UK.

It all began as a routine day. The weather had been fair, but a small and very deep low-pressure system was intensifying out in the Atlantic and we were expecting a punchy swell to arrive. Arriving at work, we could see that it had already hit and foamy tide lines were showing all around the coast. It was not very often that we would red flag the whole beach at Sennen, but this day was an exception. Nick, the head lifeguard, had no doubt it had to be done as it was apparent that the swell would last all day at the very least.

There were normally three of us who looked after Sennen beach: Nick, Jonny and myself. However, during peak weeks we would take on an extra lifeguard and this day we were four. Back then, the local surfers and lifeguards were almost one and the same thing, although as lifeguards we were paid. But other surfers would spend most of their spare time hanging around the beach or lifeguard hut; a good camaraderie was built up and they would often assist the lifeguards when necessary.

Around mid-tide on this particular day, the weather had closed in and there were only a few hardy punters on the beach. The surf was pumping and there were expectant surfers hanging about. Suddenly, the lookout spotted a rubber Zodiac inflatable boat being launched from inside Sennen harbour. We could not believe our eyes as the Zodiac nosed its way out of the harbour and blasted off, heading for the big surf in the middle of the bay! Not only that, but we counted nine people on board – none of whom appeared to be wearing life jackets! It took just seconds for the boat to reach the breaking waves, and the guy at the helm began to try and surf them. Well, it was inevitable and happened so fast: the boat broached, caught a rail, and flipped over, catapulting all nine occupants into the water.

Suddenly, all those days of chatting together, working as a team, dreaming up hand signals, being friends with the local surfers, were pulled into focus as we were forced to react. We had already pulled on our wetsuits in anticipation, but there were others – some off-duty lifeguards and surfers – who responded with no wetsuits. Dave, a lifeguard from Porthcurno beach, was in the water with us for over an hour that day and was pretty much in the early stages of hypothermia by the end of the operation.

Anyway, Nick and another guy had already sprinted for the water, carrying rescue boards and tubes. Jonny, who wasn't on duty but was fortunately on the beach, joined them immediately and paddled out to where the casualties were scattered about. Other local surfers came to help as by now the casualties – a mix of navy Wrens and some Royal Marines – were caught up in a pretty major rip. The first concern for us lifeguards was to account for all the occupants of the boat, including looking under the upturned Zodiac. That done, some of the rescuers began trying to tow casualties back to the shore, but it was proving heavy work with relentless sets of waves breaking around them. Nick and Jonny managed to start grouping the casualties together, and the upturned Zodiac, still at hand, was used as an aid for the casualties to hang on to.

The fuel cans were still attached to the boat and were proving hazardous. I had been left to direct operations from the lifeguard hut and it was at this point I saw Nick use one of the signals we had dreamt up, to call for helicopter back-up immediately. So I made the call via landline and within half an hour, a red and grey Royal Navy Sea King helicopter, the *Ace of Spades*, was on the scene and began winching the worst of the casualties into the chopper to go to hospital. I enlisted the help of another off-duty lifeguard to monitor communications and watch the beach and joined my mates in the surf to assist with bringing the rest of the casualties ashore. During the winching operation, one of the casualties, in a panic, tried to scramble for the rescue line and had to be dealt a slap by Jonny B. as there were more needy casualties to go first.

The whole rescue took well over an hour. All the occupants of the Zodiac were saved. Although a couple spent a few days in hospital, none were the worse for their terrifying experience in the surf. We were elated and buzzing for days. All those times discussing 'What if . . .' paid off in one burst that afternoon.

3

Small . . . with Massive Feet

In 2000 I became head lifeguard at Sennen Cove, Cornwall's furthest-flung beach, responsible for looking after approximately a mile and a half of beach. My life revolved around all aspects of lifeguarding and, idyllic as it was, it was also demanding and stressful. In high season with the weather set fair we could easily expect somewhere in the region of four to seven thousand holidaymakers to pitch up daily. During a typical day we would be called upon to deal with all manner of incidents, from assisting bathers in the water, carrying out both minor and major first aid, reuniting lost children with their parents, to carrying out full-on sea rescues.

There is a world of difference between our beaches here around the very tidal Land's End area (Porthcurno, Sennen and Gwynver amongst others) and – at that time – Penwith's more touristy beaches, such as Hayle and St Ives further up the coast. Sennen and in particular Gwynver face a slightly different direction and tend to pick up more swell; we would often have massive waves hitting sandbanks with huge, powerful currents swirling here and there.

These are known as rip currents and are the result of swell waves pushing lots of water over sandbanks. As the water cannot stay there it will always try to find its way back to sea and it does so, draining seaward between these banks. Getting caught in a rip tide can be powerful and alarming, even to the most experienced sea swimmer.

Further up the coast, on beaches with long stretches of sand and perhaps much less swell, and where beachgoers are more spread out, lifeguards would often have a more relaxed regime. They had the luxury of time and could concentrate on their own fitness during the working day. There were even tales of covert groups of bored life-guards creeping up on neighbouring lifeguard stations and pelting them with eggs. This, in effect, resulted in a per-ceived difference between what became known as the 'top' and 'bottom' ends.

At Sennen, our days, especially during peak weeks, were pretty full on, and my team of four lifeguards and I had to maintain our fitness levels on a personal basis as and when we could. Every day, we'd rotate between half-hour stints. For example, we'd spend thirty minutes on lookout at the hut, followed by thirty minutes on each red and yellow flag, followed by half an hour patrolling on the quad bike and carrying out first aid duties, then half an hour to relax, then back on lookout. This took dedication and teamwork from all of us. No one wanted to leave to work elsewhere, no one wanted to break up the team.

Lifeguarding involves plenty of interaction with the public and over the years that can also include a fair bit of verbal abuse. This was graphically imprinted on my mind when I had to cover for someone on one of our 'top end' beaches one day when we were short staffed. The language and level of abuse was an eye-opener, I can tell you. I was told to 'Eff off' more than once. Back on Sennen, I breathed a sigh of relief and gave a silent nod of respect to those lifeguard colleagues who had to tolerate this sort of behaviour on a daily basis.

During the sixties and seventies our beaches around Land's End used to attract both serious surfers and also those interested in the flora and fauna and in walking the spectacular cliff paths steeped in wrecking legend. This was the end of the line; you had to be really determined to come all this way for your holiday. Visitors *wanted* to come here, rather than finding themselves here by accident. It is fair to say that by the time they had driven as far as Newquay, the vast majority of tourists had more than likely been on the road for many hours and were at their wits' end with the kids going bonkers in the back of the car.

In those days, road travel through rural Cornwall was a very sedate affair and the sooner the visitor accepted 'drekly' time, as the locals call it, the better! Roads were narrow and constructed around fields rather than through them, resulting in lots of corners and very few long stretches for any overtaking manoeuvres. They would jam up with cars breaking down and caravans with flat tyres. It was chaos. I remember one summer day in the seventies driving from Camborne to Penzance, approximately ten miles, a journey that would normally take thirty to forty minutes but on that day took over three hours! So you can see why the area of north Cornwall around Newquay was and still is very popular for holidaymakers but Land's End, being a good couple of hours' drive away, tends to be a bit quieter.

I didn't like to leave Sennen if I could avoid it because apart from anything else I felt duty-bound to be there. I did, however, have to go to St Ives from time to time, as that was where our depot was based. Twice a week during the lifeguarding season we also had early-morning swim training sessions there and myself and Lloyd (my pal and fellow supervisor) would usually pop into the depot afterwards to pick up supplies or have a meeting. We were always keen to get in and get out and head back to work as quickly as possible and on one morning in August 2003, close to the end of the season, I was about to do just that when our boss pitched up.

'Look what I've got here,' he said proudly, pointing behind him to where a small furry brown ball came pattering through the door. Its walk was disjointed, as if it had no control over its limbs. Despite its small size, I couldn't help but notice that it had massive feet. 'His name's Bilbo and he's a Newfoundland,' he said. 'I've just bought him – what do you think?'

Well, he was gorgeous! He was the cutest thing I'd ever seen. He had the most beautiful amber eyes, a little brown nose and tufty fur on his head that looked a bit like a bearskin hat. He was fourteen weeks old and very excited, rushing around, sliding on the floor and crashing into furniture. He was hilarious to watch as he went around meeting everyone. He rushed over to me, and when I picked him up he felt like a complete ball of energy, unable to contain himself. Even though I had no intention of owning a dog, I could not help thinking: I would love to train something like you, my lad.

After that, whenever he came to the depot he would

come to me, snuffling and wagging his whole body. He and I connected right from the start and although he left my side every now and again to investigate some sound or other, he would inevitably come back and sit by me. Bilbo was immediately popular with us lifeguards because he was such a scream. He sloped in with those huge feet and his legs going in four different directions at once and people either cracked up laughing or fell in love with him. And of course he wanted to be everybody's friend. I have always felt a connection to animals, but must admit that I had never specially considered myself to be a dog person until then. And I was certainly not expecting to fall in love with him. I had no intention of that at all. I mean, I liked him, but that was as far as it went. Or so I thought.

Out of all the guys in the depot, he hung out with me the most. One day, as I was mucking around with him, I whispered in his ear, 'My boy, *MY* boy.' He looked up at me and shuffled closer, flapping his bushy tail, and from then on, even though he didn't belong to me, he was 'my boy'. During the months that followed, Bilbo's owner would have to attend meetings and increasingly he'd say to me: 'J'mo, would you look after Bilbo for me?' He himself had been a lifeguard but was doing more of a desk job, so he wasn't on the beach at that point. And I was happy to look after his dog for him because we got on really well, Bilbo and me.

The St Ives depot was a massive old Nissen hut, one of those big corrugated buildings with a large roller door, which was open to the elements most of the time. It had loads of rooms in it but no doors, so there were all these dark areas that you could go and hide in. So, of course, when I was looking after Bilbo, we played hide and seek. I developed this special five-note whistle for him that he latched on to immediately. He would realize it was me, and we'd play for hours on end. He couldn't see me in the dark unless I moved, and as there was no wind blowing through he didn't seem able to get a scent of me either. He'd be standing around and I'd see his head go from side to side as he listened, and he'd plod off somewhere else. And then I'd whistle and he'd come back, eventually finding me. It was a bit of fun and very playful, but looking back we actually formed a bond very early. We just clicked.

We used to cook up a big batch of porridge at work for our breakfast. There was a chair in the hut that was lower than all the others, and – on the basis that he was the smallest – Lloyd would always sit on it to have his porridge. One day, Bilbo, who was seventeen months old and already growing to quite a size, put his paws on Lloyd's shoulders and started pushing the wheeled chair all round the office. It was really comical to watch and, once Bilbo saw that we all enjoyed his prank, it became a regular occurrence. Lloyd would be saying, 'Gerrof, Bilbo, you lummox!' while everyone else cracked up. Bilbo in the meantime was having none of it and slobbered all over him, often with him pinioned against the wall or a piece of furniture. He seemed to love winding Lloyd up, even snaffling his breakfast one time.

It was obvious right from the start that Bilbo liked the environment of the depot, the openness of it, and the yard. But most of all, he liked being with people. It also gave him the opportunity for his first romance. One day he just vanished into thin air. He wasn't in the yard so Lloyd jumped in the car and drove around the neighbouring streets looking for him. He found that he had sneaked off down the road outside the depot – thankfully not a busy one – past the rugby club, and all the way down the hill to see the fluffy Samoyed bitch that belonged to the girl who worked in the local chemists. Not long afterwards he repeated the trick. It would be the first of many disappearing acts and scrapes that Bilbo, aka 'the love god', would get into when it came to his pursuit of the fairer sex.

He was a sly one at times, make no mistake. He was extremely observant and when we were out in the 4x4 and he spied a dog out of the window, I think he made a mental note of it and would try to go and see them if he got the opportunity. Perhaps it was because of his lack of interaction with other dogs day-to-day that they were a constant source of interest to him. But it was clear from the start that Bilbo definitely had a calling for the wild. He wanted to be out and free – he didn't want to be cooped up.

The first time I took Bilbo to the beach was in the autumn of 2004 when he was around eighteen months old and hanging out with us a lot at the depot. Part of our remit from Penwith Council was for the lifeguard service to assist in cleaning up the beaches in the winter when all the tourists had long gone home. As well as litter we had to remove dead seals and cetaceans – dolphins mainly – that got washed up on the beach. There was a lot of monofilament netting being used at one time and dolphins could become entangled in these 'invisible' nets and drown. Fishermen could do nothing other than cut them out and dump them, and some of the carcasses would end up washed up on our beaches in the south-west. Collecting them wasn't a nice job either but if you left them they would just rot there, stinking, making it unpleasant for everybody.

Lloyd and I used a quad bike to collect the animals and we took Bilbo beach cleaning with us. He came to recognize when we turned into the car park and saw the sand dunes, as that was one of his walking spots. He would start whining, quickly morphing into full-on yelping with excitement at the prospect of a swim in the sea, which he could scent in his nostrils. He was usually in the back of my vehicle and many a time I had to try and calm him before letting him out. 'Now look here, Billy,' I'd begin, but he wasn't listening. He was still very young and full of beans. Just holding him close until we could scope out the beach was an exercise in itself. He would then bound off down the steep dunes so fast that his body would overtake his legs and there would be this almighty explosion of sand, limbs and brown fur as he slid to a clumsy stop, tail still wagging. To be honest, he was more of a hindrance than a help when it came to beach cleaning. If we were collecting a dead seal, for example, he would get very involved in sniffing and rolling in it. Afterwards, he'd stink to high heaven, but Bilbo obviously thought eau de rotting seal was pure catnip to the ladies or something, because he looked very pleased with himself. In the end it was safer to leave him behind on those days, otherwise we would spend the next few hours trying to clean him up while he reeked out the depot.

One winter's day we were cleaning on Sennen and it was virtually deserted apart from a woman with a child and a dog. The child was no more than a toddler and was wearing a red padded suit – a little onesie thing made from fluffy down. The tide was out and Lloyd and I were at the top of the beach below the lifeguard hut picking up litter and stuff and the kiddie was about two-thirds of the way down. Maybe it was the strange shape of his suit but whatever it was, it was like a red rag to a bull. All of a sudden Bilbo was alert. His eyes looked at the kid and then looked at us and I could tell he was thinking: What the hell's that? I've never seen one of them before. And with that he took off at full pelt. He just bolted, with me shouting at the top of my voice: 'Noooo, Bilbo!' The next thing I saw was Bilbo flying through the air with both front legs extended in front of him. It was like one of those slow-motion comedy sketches – except no one was laughing. Then, *WOP!*, he connected with the child and *BOOF!*, like a small explosion they both went up in the air!

By now the kid's mother had started running towards him and I thought: Oh God, we're in the shit now. Lloyd had gone pale and said, 'J'mo, I'm not going down there – you'll have to go.' So I ran down, expecting a right rollicking at the very least. Fortunately though, the woman was one of those easy-going bohemian types and was actually all right about it. (Phew!) The boy was covered in wet sand, but was otherwise unharmed. Even so, a lot of parents would have kicked up a real fuss and it could have been the end of Bilbo as far as being allowed on the beach was concerned.

'That dog's wild – he flipping pulled me over the other day,' Lloyd complained when I arrived back with Bilbo. He had recently been dog-sitting Bilbo and had taken him to Porthkidney beach, near St Ives. But Bilbo had yanked on the lead so hard Lloyd had ended up flat on his back on the sand and had to let him go. He could see Bilbo in the distance but stood no chance of being able to catch up with him. He got him back eventually, but declared Bilbo 'too hyperactive' to look after again. Lloyd had had enough and realized there was no way he could control him.

While I saw the humorous side of Bilbo's unruly behaviour (especially where Lloyd was concerned), at twelve months he was getting to the point where he was nearly fully grown, as strong as anything, and equipped with very sharp teeth. One day at the depot, Bilbo lay in the doorway, minding his own business, chewing on a rawhide bone. One of the young lifeguards decided to steal it from him for a laugh. He got down on all fours and made as if to pick up the chew with his teeth. Bilbo saw him trying to take his bone and almost sliced the top of his ear in half. Luckily we had full trauma kits at the depot and patched the chap up. He was OK, but in much pain for an hour or two. That was when I realized just how incredibly sharp Bilbo's teeth were. Like bears' teeth, with massive incisors that could easily tear flesh. It was a daft thing for anyone to do: Bilbo would never have attacked him except for the fact that he was making noises like a dog – and he *was* trying to steal his bone after all ...

One day, Bilbo's owners took him for a walk on the dunes at Hayle. There was a woman jogging in the distance and, spotting her, Bilbo took off after her like a guided missile. She didn't see him until the last second when he appeared from the dunes like a grizzly – jumping out of the long marram grass and knocking her flying. She went completely berserk, and quite rightly too. It was worrying and was also, I felt, a warning sign for the poor guy. I could imagine Bilbo chasing sheep and being shot by a farmer, which was a distinct possibility in deepest Cornwall, or that he might even bite someone and things could get really serious. One thing was becoming obvious to me: if Bilbo got really out of control, he could easily end up having to be put down. What's more, I realized I cared deeply about what happened to him.

As the months passed, Bilbo filled out and by twelve months he was already quite large, weighing in at about four to five stone and showing more signs of disobedience. Personally, I felt that he was not receiving the attention he needed to be under effective control because his owners simply did not have the time to look after such a boisterous dog. I was already concerned that this dog was either going to become totally out of control, or maybe be adopted by someone who just wanted him as a fashion accessory. It beggars belief that some people would own a dog purely to follow a trend but as the animal rescue centres will attest, it happens all too often. Lots of people used to say to me, 'I bet he's a real chick magnet.' And I'd look at them incredulously, thinking, Do you *really* think so? Do you think that any girl who is all dressed up is going to let this huge, slobbery dog anywhere near her? I don't think so!

As Bilbo got bigger, my boss stopped bringing him to work. It played on my mind, wondering how Bilbo was feeling. I'd cared for him more than anyone had over the past few months, but he wasn't mine, and there was nothing I could do. For the rest of that winter the depot was quiet and subdued. Things just weren't the same without him.

4

A Twelve-Stone Alarm Clock

Spring came, and when Bilbo was about to turn two, I went to see my boss at his house to deliver some paperwork. Bilbo was on his own in the garden and although I hadn't seen him for ages he clearly remembered me. He saw me coming down the drive and went nuts, jumping around and trying to climb over the top of the fence to get to me. He couldn't because it was too high, but he managed to get himself onto the top of it and then of course he got stuck. One of his huge hairy legs slipped down between the slats of the fence and he was precariously balanced there, all gangly, and yelping excitedly as I helped him down.

I felt so sorry for him, left there in the garden all day alone. Well, not exactly all alone; his owners weren't cruel to him in that they gave him food and water and had taken him to training classes and to the grooming parlour. But although they had an extensive garden, dogs don't normally exercise themselves. So Bilbo just sat with his face looking out through the bars of the gate. And he was there most days, on his own.

Anyway, that Monday in May my heart went out to him

and I suggested to his owner that maybe, now and again, I could take him to work with me for a day. I hated to think of him being all alone for hours on end and if Bilbo could accompany me it would give me some companionship and him a break from the garden. He readily agreed and Bilbo began to spend a day at a time with me, riding in the 4x4 and walking the coastal paths. Most of the time it was just the two of us.

Walking Bilbo was quite an experience for anyone not used to walking large dogs – especially unneutered males! It was certainly an eye-opener for me, with a steep learning curve. Most who tried were astounded at his power. Statistically Newfoundlands are, pound for pound, the world's strongest dog. Bilbo had never really got the opportunity to interact fully with other dogs when he should have. The first months of a dog's life are crucial in terms of socializing with other dogs and different animals, but Bilbo had done very little of that. As a result he wasn't that keen on other dogs, especially other males.

Bilbo loved the freedom of being out of that garden. He bounded along the coastal paths ahead of me, through the gorse and the clover, tail wagging, but he didn't run away – he stuck close to me and we had a great time together. It seemed he associated me with having an interesting time and he never wandered far from my side.

Up until this point, Bilbo and I were just good friends, but it was when his owners went away for a few days and he came to stay with me at Chez Noir that we really bonded. It was just four days in all, but they were four days that changed my life. I picked him up one Monday night, along with 'a few of his things'. These included a food bowl the size of a bucket, a massive water bowl, a stand to put them in, a sack of food, a bag of towels, a great big hide chew – everything was HUGE. Having unloaded all this into Chez Noir, and with a *very* excited Bilbo in residence, I suddenly realized that my place, which had always seemed spacious enough, was a lot smaller than I had previously imagined!

Well, the next four days, although working days, were full of fun and laughter for both of us – albeit they required a bit of 'adjustment' for me. Having never had a dog to look after, I was straight in at the deep end with Bilbo. His sheer size alone was a bit intimidating, to be honest. He didn't leave my side after getting out of the car, but in an hour or so he grew curious and began exploring the large garden surrounding Chez Noir. The main house, back from mine, had only a cat in situ so Bilbo was able to start marking out his own patch with no opposition from other dogs. He reappeared every now and then to check that I was still inside and, happy that I was, he would disappear again.

He slept well at night but Bilbo, I quickly discovered, was an early riser. In fact, it was barely first light when I heard him stirring in the kitchen, having a noisy drink of water. Then there was the sound of him batting the kitchen door open and – *pad, pad, pad* – he lumbered into the bedroom. Through eyes still half closed with sleep, I saw him sit down beside my bed, letting out a great sigh as he did so. Not fancying getting up just yet, I pretended to be asleep and, getting no response from me, he began a sort of squeak-cum-pathetic-half-bark routine, which ended with a stamping of feet, followed by a full-on assault of the bed. His message – hardly subtle – was received loud and clear by me: it was time to get up! I fussed him for a little while before having to push him out of the way to make room to get dressed (Bilbo, I also discovered, loved to get *real* close!).

I had no idea what food was best for his coat and general well-being; I only had the bag of dried food he had come with. When it was time to feed him that first evening, I called him and he came in through the door, tail wagging. 'Hello, my boy,' I said. 'Are you ready for your supper?' I placed his bowl of dried food down for him, but he refused to eat. Instead he gave me this doleful look, as if to say, 'I'm not eating that. In fact I'm not even hungry.'

Well, I let it go the first couple of days, putting it down to the excitement of being in new surroundings. Getting him to drink water was not a problem, but by day three he had still not eaten anything and so I had to have a chat with him. 'Look, my lad, you have to understand that life for us has changed, especially for you,' I explained as he sat looking at me. 'From now on we will eat at the same time.' I knew that he was partial to raw eggs and so, that evening, while cooking my supper, I prepared Bilbo's too, mixing his dried food with a couple of raw eggs. Perhaps it was the aroma of my cooking but Bilbo kept his eyes firmly on the stove, looking at me every now and again as if to say, 'May I have some of that too, please?' And so, having eaten my dinner, I mixed up my leftovers with Bilbo's supper and began feeding it to him with a wooden spoon, a bit at a time. Billy loved it, and it showed in his eyes as he ate *all* of his supper that evening. All the while I would be looking at him and saying to him encouragingly, 'What a good boy you are, my lovely Bilbo, *my* Bilbo.' Quite a lot of our day-to-day communication was by eye contact and hand signals. Bilbo had incredible eyes and could tell me so much.

But of course he wasn't *my* Bilbo and as the week went on and Friday drew nearer I began to dread the moment I would have to take him home. He just seemed so much happier when he was with me. But of course he wasn't my dog and it wasn't my decision.

Bilbo clearly felt the same because when we arrived at his owners' house, he wouldn't even get out of the car. Eventually, after much wrangling, my boss and I pulled him out. After handing him back, I slipped away as quietly as I could, trying to leave with the minimum of fuss so as not to upset Bilbo. But as I looked back I saw from the confused look in his eyes that he wanted to come with me. I felt awful as I drove away. 'Well, I will have him again next week,' I told myself. Even so, that night and all of the next day I felt out of sorts. I went through my usual routines, but all the while I felt like I was forgetting something. Eventually it dawned on me what the matter was – I was missing the big fella. No, more than that, I was actually *pining* for him! And, as it turned out, I was not the only one who couldn't settle that weekend.

On Sunday morning my boss rang. He sounded shattered. 'J'mo, mate, we're at our wits' end. Bilbo won't stop howling. We've barely slept, he won't eat, he's got an upset tummy and he's keeping us awake all night.' There was a pause. 'Do you think . . . Would you consider letting Bilbo live with you permanently?'

My heart leapt. I was only too happy to have him; the two of us had already formed quite a bond. But I insisted that if I was going to take him on full time it had to be on my terms. 'I'll take him but on one condition: he'll be with me all the time, including at work. In the winter he's going to be in the office with me, and in the summer he's going to be on the beach with me.' I was adamant that I would never let him be on his own again. It was agreed and I went and collected him straight away, driving as fast as I dared.

I could hear Bilbo's howling from the end of the drive, but as soon as he saw me, he stopped, tail wagging. It was almost as if he'd always known I'd come back. My boss said goodbye to him, with a combination of sadness and relief, and with that, Bilbo hopped in the back of my car. At last, he really was my boy! We got home, and Bilbo ran through the door and headed straight for his spot. Grabbing him in a bear hug, I made Bilbo the same promise I'd made to his owner on the phone: 'You're my boy. And I won't ever leave you. Not ever.'

Those first days following Bilbo's return to Chez Noir were new, thrilling, alarming and exhausting all at the same time. Bilbo was so very excited, now that he had my undivided attention, and was making the most of having me to himself. I too was learning just how to cope with such a potentially messy creature. I soon understood that the towels his owner had sent with him were to put around his drinking stand, for example.

After we'd had breakfast, I took him out for what would become our regular walk. It was vaguely circular and would normally take us about an hour – a wonderful start to the day. On the way he would encounter scents so strong that even *I* could smell them. The recent smell of a dog fox for example. As we went from hill to hill and field to field, we would bump into all sorts of creatures, as well as people on horseback; worst of all were marauding herds of heifers who always seemed *very* interested in Bilbo. Quite often we had to 'leg it' quickly as, judging by the angry look on their faces, I sensed they might be about to charge us! Because our walks were off the beaten track, Bilbo got into the habit of backing himself up, well into the gorse or bracken, to do his 'business'. And should he ever be caught short, I always carried a trusty spade with which to dispatch the offending mess into the thick undergrowth.

We would also bump into local characters either on their way to work or just walking their own dogs and some-times we chatted for so long that Bilbo would just give up and lie down, doing his inimitable '*Not again!*' sigh. Aware-ness and control are paramount and are intuitive to me as a lifeguard so I was constantly looking around and ahead for other dog walkers, dogs on the loose, or just animals in general. Not that Bilbo was seeking mischief, but better to be aware and 'rather safe than sorry' – that was how I saw it. With that in mind, I always tried to take Bilbo for his walks at the same time each day, sticking to a routine. This also helped with timing apropos meeting others with big or problematic dogs. Our routes would vary depending on the time of year, as there are always many more dogs here during the summer months.

Back home, Billy headed for the stream where I had dammed a small area for him so he could lie down in the cool water. He would often be in there for anything up to ten minutes before taking up his usual 'on guard' position under the bush outside the kitchen door, awaiting his breakfast. There was a footpath that ran behind the prop-erty between a camp site and Sennen beach. Quite often, as

I was cooking up some scrambled eggs for Bilbo's breakfast, I heard children shouting, 'There he is, that's him. That's Bilbo!'

Because it was just the two of us I was extremely sensitive to how he was feeling. Not that he wasn't good at letting it be known if he was displeased. I soon learnt his language. He had a curious half-bark, half-whine he would make to get my attention. If that did not get a result, he would start stamping on the floor, eventually getting up and standing over me. It might be a case of him trying to tell me, 'Hey, Capt, there's water in my bowl but it's no longer fresh.' Or, 'May I please go outside and guard my kingdom?'

Bilbo knew that I wasn't going to leave him, because I would tell him so all the time. I never left him at home on his own, even for a couple of hours. So, when I went for my weekly food shop, he came with me. He was a bit too crazy to come in the shop, so I decided to leave him in the car with the windows open, and he was as good as gold.

On Monday morning, instead of driving to work alone, I had company. Lloyd and I went for our training swim down at Porthmeor beach, near the Tate Gallery in St Ives. I knew Bilbo would follow me into the water, and it might be difficult to keep an eye on him because we were doing drills.

'He'll be all right in the car while we swim, J'mo, it's not warm today,' Lloyd said.

Begrudgingly, I left him there. It was a sunny spring day; still cold enough that there weren't many other people about but the beach was at its prettiest. We set off on our swim. We'd got almost as far as the first buoy when I heard splashing and huffing behind me. I looked around and there

Bilbo was! Chuffing away like a steam engine! I noticed that he did not swim doggy paddle like most dogs, but had more of a canine breaststroke. He looked so happy, paddling along, and it was clear that, like me, he was meant for the water.

A few weeks later I was supervising some youngsters while they were surfing and had left Bilbo in the car. The next thing I knew, he was there beside us. I'd only left a window open enough for him to get his head out, but despite being almost fully grown (i.e. enormous) he'd obviously managed to squeeze everything out. But then he wasn't as chunky as he looked. His fur made him appear larger but when he was wet you could see how buff he actually was – there was no fat on *my* boy!

Bilbo had been named after the J. R. R. Tolkien character Bilbo Baggins from *The Hobbit*, but once he started working on the beach with me it was agreed that although he had hairy feet, he was definitely *not* a hobbit. I preferred to relate his name to one of the first surfboard companies in Cornwall. Two guys, Bill Bailey and Bob Head, formed Bilbo Surfing Co. combining both their first names. In fact the original Bilbo surfboards are now highly sought after.

And so we developed a routine; a life together. I got to know him, and he got to know me. We slotted in together really easily, Bilbo and me. Although until I got used to it, I would be jolted awake every morning by a giant paw plonked on my face. Because my bed was on the same level as Bilbo's shoulders he would just wander in and if I wasn't awake he'd put his paw on my face, which usually did the trick! Quite often I'd go in to work with great scratches on the side of my face and they'd ask, 'What have you been up to, J'mo?' and I'd point at Bilbo and say, 'Him.' But it was only his way of saying 'Good morning' and I couldn't be cross with him because he was just so endearing.

He had his own mannerisms. I noticed that his eyebrows worked independently and he would wiggle them when he was getting impatient. Or he'd puff up his cheeks with air and let it out in a theatrical fashion, as if to say, 'I'm soooo bored.' I came to believe that dogs really do smile, because when Bilbo came in to see me first thing in the morning, having biffed me on the head, he would scrunch his face up into what looked for all the world like a smile. He'd sit in front of me and I'd ask: 'Where's my kiss for the day?' and he'd give me a big slobbery one. It was a full-on love fest – so much for me not being a dog person! For my part I found I enjoyed having another soul around the house.

That's not to say of course that he wasn't a handful. Bilbo had been taken to a few training classes as a small puppy and he knew basic commands like 'Sit'. He knew his name but I soon found that he wouldn't stay, or come on command. I began to read up about dogs and learnt that larger breeds take longer to reach maturity than small dogs. That certainly seemed to be true for Bilbo, as I couldn't do anything with him when I first got him because he was so scatty. But while he was not grown up mentally, he had matured physically and was extremely strong. That summer, my cousin, who grew up in Edinburgh, came to stay and she bent down to Bilbo and said: 'Och, aren't you sweet, give me a kiss.'

I said to her: 'Don't bend down to him like that because if he moves his head up he could knock you out.'

But she said, 'No he won't,' and put her head down for

a kiss and of course he did exactly that. I heard a crack and then it was just like claret everywhere – blood all down her face. It didn't break her nose luckily but she was pretty smacked up. I felt bad for her, but while you've got to show an animal like that who's in charge, you also have to show them some respect.

The biggest problem to start with was that my front room was very small – only three metres square – and my table was just a low coffee table. Bilbo lay on the floor and if I got up for any reason he would instantly get up as if to say, 'Where are we going?' occasionally knocking the table over in the process. One summer's evening, I laid out some plates and glasses because my neighbour Leroy was coming round for a beer. But Bilbo was so pleased when he saw that we had company, his wagging tail swept everything off the table and onto the floor.

He wasn't at all obedient. In fact he was simply terrible. I used to sit in my place, head in hands, thinking: What the hell have I done? I'd made a commitment, and I would never back out on that, but I just couldn't see how this could go on. He was getting bigger and bigger. One day I was in just that position, trying to figure out the best way to control him, when he barged into the room, flinging the door open with a bang. He sat in front of me, raised his huge leg and pawed me on the side of the head. 'I want attention!'

'Ouch, you mutt!' I exploded. 'That hurt.' He just looked at me and then tried to do it again. Catching hold of his leg, I looked into his eyes and said, 'You and I must have a chat, my lad . . . *you* do as *I* say, and not the other way round, get it?'

He looked at me, dolefully, and went and sat on his bed.

From that point on, I was determined. I didn't want to give him up. I had to show him that I was in charge. Over the next few weeks, every time Bilbo challenged me, I would speak to him, firmly. He was still a young puppy though, and at times it seemed like it just wouldn't sink in. It all culminated with Bilbo and me sorting out the pack leader 'issue' in the garden at Chez Noir. We were rolling around outside together, play-fighting, then suddenly it changed into something more aggressive. He was trying to throw his weight around – and he was a big dog; he weighed nearly twelve stone, which is almost as heavy as me. I just thought, I'm not having that, and, grappling on the floor, I admit I had to deliver a slap to get him to stop.

After this incident we settled down with much more respect for each other. I'd heard that in the wild, the top dog in the pack sometimes grabs lesser dogs by the jowls with its teeth for a moment or two. It's a way of exercising dominance over them, apparently, and I decided to do that with Bilbo. I grabbed him by the cheek with my teeth and made a gentle, growling sound. Bilbo just sat there looking at me; he accepted it. It's a way of showing them that you're in charge and you're letting them know that. However, I would not recommend trying that one out on your neighbour's Rottweiler!

Once I'd addressed the balance of power, he was fine. I think he appreciated that I'd rescued him from his loneliness, so he didn't give me a lot of grief. If he hadn't come to live with me, however, I think the outcome could have been very different for Bilbo. As he'd shown when he frightened that woman on the dunes at Hayle, you just couldn't have a dog his size running around out of control. He needed firm, consistent handling, and I was the man for the job.

5

Gentle Giant

Bilbo had been bred locally, in Penzance. He had brothers and sisters who were black like their parents but Bilbo and one sister were special because they were the only chocolate-coloured ones in the litter. He came from a well-known line of pedigree Newfoundlands somewhere in the South-ampton area, whose kennel name was Blackansand. His sire was Blackansand Major Tom and his dam was Blackansand Dilly Dally.

I knew he came from a strong line because he had the most fantastic temperament. He was a very laid-back dog and people were amazed how quiet he could be. Despite his size, you would never know he was there half the time. He would just lie quietly. Until another dog came in, that is – and then he'd be up moving and pacing around. But as a rule, he was really cool – everybody remarked on how laid-back he was. I do firmly believe that a pet's demeanour is governed by the relationship they have with their owners. I used to house- and pet-sit for people, and I would always see that when the animals weren't relaxed it was because the owners weren't either. It was often upsetting if it was a long job, because just as the pets were beginning to relax I would leave.

Despite his gentle nature, some people were wary of allowing Bilbo into their homes because of his size. If he walked into your house, for example, you would tend to know about it afterwards. His underside could often be muddy and damp and would dry as he lay on the floor, so when he got up there would be this dusty shadow of a dog. It was a bit like a police outline of a body! Most cat-owners didn't want him coming into their house at all as the cats would simply freak out when they first saw him! Actually, he would never attack a cat, but most people simply didn't want to take the risk. I lost quite a few house-sitting jobs once I adopted Bilbo. One of the families I used to house-sit for had a long-haired Alsatian bitch in residence and the first thing Bilbo did when I took him in there was to cock his leg and wee all over their settee. Right in front of everybody too! So it was a case of, 'He's not coming in here anymore!'

I couldn't really blame them, but worse was to happen when I was looking after a fairly new house in Sennen. I had gone over to a nearby pub called the Logan Rock with Bilbo and a friend of mine and we were all in the bar having a few beers. I was chatting to the barman when I felt Bilbo pulling on his lead. I turned round and saw that he was chewing something. 'What has he just eaten?' I asked my mate and he replied: 'Oh, that gentleman just offered him his bones after his meal.' 'Bones? What bones?' I said. 'Oh, just some lamb bones.' I felt rather annoyed but there are lots of people who are ignorant of the fact that although *some* cooked bones are OK, such as beef or pork bones,

chicken – and especially lamb – bones are a definite no-no.
Chicken and lamb bones tend to splinter and in the worst
scenario could actually kill a dog. But it was too late to do
anything about it as Bilbo had already scoffed the lot. Later
we went back to the house and I bedded Bilbo down in
their large porch for the night.

The porch had a large coconut mat in it, which Bilbo
found rather comfy. However, when I came down in the
morning I saw that the poor guy must have had a terrible
tummy ache during the night and although he had tried his
best to hold it in, the evidence was everywhere! My fault,
as I should have known and checked on him. As soon as I
let him outside he immediately backed into the bushes and
was really unwell. The poor chap was beside himself with
embarrassment. Rather than coming to me with his usual
grin, he hung his head and for once his tail wasn't wagging.
His eyes said it all: 'Sorry, boss.' I felt awful for him too. He
spent the next few days on a diet of boiled chicken and rice,
and was soon back to normal.

But that regrettable incident aside, Bilbo had his own
reasons to be enthusiastic about our house-sitting jobs. Chez
Noir had never been assembled with permanent accommodation in mind. It had been used as a summerhouse for the
landlord's children and the occasional family visitor and
consequently there was not a lot of room for furniture –
especially for larger items such as a settee. Bilbo had not
been allowed on the furniture by his previous owners and
of course when he came to live with me there was no comfy
seat big enough for him there either. So, as I discovered
much later, on the rare occasion when we had to spend a
night at someone else's house, Bilbo would go on patrol

once everyone was asleep and pad around until he found the most comfortable settee, whereupon he would climb aboard. The trouble was, because it was *so* comfy, he would often oversleep and be discovered in the morning with a guilty 'Who, me?' look on his face. He was even caught one morning asleep on a settee with the family cat sitting on a cushion just above him, one paw resting on his shoulder!

Like all puppies, Bilbo was inquisitive and just wanted to find out what things were. I never used to put him on the lead because he didn't run away. But one day we were out walking around Chapel Carn Brea when I lost him. Chapel Carn Brea is the most westerly hill in Cornwall and is a distinctive pudding-basin shape, about two miles from where we lived. It's an important historical site owned by the National Trust and, at 198 metres above sea level, the views are breathtaking. It was a Bronze Age burial site and was where they lit the first beacon to warn that the Spanish Armada was coming – in fact they still light a beacon on it every June to celebrate the summer solstice.

Bilbo must have been about two at the time and had barely been out of my sight. When I realized he was nowhere to be seen, my heart started beating that much faster. I tried not to panic, and tried not to think about what life might be like if he didn't return, but my heart pounded.

'Bilbo! Bilbo, come here!' I called and called for him until my throat was sore. Then, I looked down the hill and saw that down at the bottom he had cornered two sheep. They had jumped up on top of the hedge and Bilbo was standing below, looking at them as if to say, 'What are you?' I had to get down there quickly because I didn't want the farmer to think he was going to attack the sheep and shoot him. There were plenty of signs saying as much: 'Any dogs found worrying the sheep will be shot!' I knew he was just curious but, given his size, I'm not sure the farmer would agree.

I took a wonderful photo of Bilbo standing benignly next to this sign, with the sheep looking at him quizzically through the gate as if to say, 'Please don't worry!' There were also some grazing Dartmoor ponies at Chapel Carn Brea and when we bumped into them Bilbo would often, having had a sniff himself, lie down on his back, put his legs in the air and let the horses come and smell him.

Considering his size, he was very gentle with the wild-life. Apart from mice, that is. Or, rather, one poor unfortunate mouse. At one time I had thought to buy a cat when we lived at Chez Noir. Being a very old and run-down collection of smaller sheds, it was easy access for all sorts of creatures. Mice of course were a constant pest, especially during the winter months. Many times pre-Bilbo, upon returning from holiday for example, I would find a family of mice had moved in amongst my clothes. I also used to find snails and slugs inside, and even a toad or two in the primitive shower area. However, when Bilbo came to stay he did not want to share me with anyone or anything and that included mice! One evening he heard one scratching around in the kitchen. I could see him becoming more agitated and stomping his feet on the wooden floor, the way he often did when he wanted attention. I moved a box to one side and like lightning Bilbo shot into the space and killed the mouse with one quick bite! No more need for a cat – the rodent problem had vanished overnight!

The chickens at Chez Noir also intrigued Bilbo, and he

soon realized that was where his breakfast came from. Not the chickens, I hasten to add, but their eggs. I cooked up the previous night's vegetable peelings, mixed them with any old bread and some rolled oats, and he and I would head for the chicken coop, where already there would be a fierce clucking coming from within. Clucking that would abruptly cease as soon as the birds sensed Bilbo was outside. I would let them out and Bilbo watched as they rushed around, catching insects unaware in their beaks or running to get a morning drink. Bilbo was very interested in looking into the egg-laying boxes, much to the disdain and alarm of any roosting chicken! He always wanted to have a good 'snuffle' at the eggs too. Once the chickens realized he was not inter-ested in chasing them, however, they relaxed and it was lovely to see them together. They wandered up the garden to Chez Noir, even strutting into the kitchen, but Bilbo wasn't too keen on that as it was *his* domain and he would usually stick his great head inside as if to say: 'Oi! You! Out!' Exit chicken.

Of course being a dog, he wasn't averse to a spot of scavenging if the opportunity presented itself. If little kid-dies on the beach happened to drop their ice creams at his feet, or wave them too close to his nose, he was more than happy to vacuum them up. He loved things that he wasn't supposed to eat, things like chocolate and grapes (I wouldn't let him have them), but I only found out about cheese much later. He loved lasagne – he would just go mental for lasagne!

Apparently one of the attractions of the brown New-foundlands is that they don't tend to have those awful bootlaces of drool hanging from their mouths like the black ones often do. And Bilbo wasn't very drooly at all. The only times he would slobber was when he was drinking or if he could smell roast chicken (or lasagne). Then it would start to flow, long tendrils of the stuff hanging from the corners of his mouth. It's surprising how fast some women can move away at the sight of drool!

His head was so big it would be on a level with the table but even if there was a cooked chicken there, he wouldn't touch it. He'd sit and look at it, but that's all. Not that he ate that much actually. By the time he was fully grown he weighed about twelve and a half stone but for a big dog he didn't really eat a huge amount of food.

The spoon-feeding went on until I said to him one evening, 'I'm sorry, Billy, but this has really got to stop, people are beginning to talk!' He just looked at me, and put his great paw on my leg as if to say, 'Just feed me another spoonful, Capt.' So I continued for a bit longer until I began to mix his dried food with things like mackerel, pilchards or shredded cooked chicken. That made meals more interesting for him. Eventually. It took a few months, but in the end he was weaned off the spoon, although ever afterwards if he felt a tad under the weather, he would insist on being spoon-fed.

For breakfast he might have some cereal with yoghurt or scrambled eggs and for lunch I'd give him some of his dried dog food, mixed with a smoked mackerel or a raw egg to keep his coat shiny. In the evening I'd offer him a bowl of his special dried food with some cooked chicken and of course water, plenty of water. Billy was really fussy about his drinks – it had to be water and it had to be fresh! It became obvious early on that he preferred to eat little and often – which is probably a good philosophy for many of us humans as well. He was actually quite delicate with his eating. He used to eat apples by taking tiny bites out of them with his little nippy teeth. A child could give him something to eat and as long as I said, 'Be gentle, Bilbo,' he would be OK.

Neither did he smell – he was really good like that. Somebody said to me once that unhappy dogs smell but a happy dog doesn't. And when I first picked Bilbo up I sensed that he was stressed and sometimes he did pong a bit, but as he settled into life at Chez Noir, his body settled too.

Even though he was a large dog, Bilbo didn't need as much exercise as one might think. A smaller dog like a Jack Russell actually needs far more, but I didn't know that at first. Before I got him I used to run two or three times a week to keep in shape. I'd run to work from where I lived in St Just, which was about five or six miles away, and then run back in the evenings. And when I first had Bilbo I took him on a couple of five-mile runs but I quickly noticed that the next day he wouldn't be fit for anything. It was just too much for him. I only did it two or three times because I realized he was tired. After that we concentrated more on walking on the sand dunes.

When he was training with me on the beach I would walk him up and down the dunes. One of our 'rules' was that no lifeguard walked up the dunes to the hut – you had to jog up. Bilbo would be jogging up there with us and I realized that was much better for him than endurance running. And that's when he started to build muscle and get much stronger.

As the summer finished and we moved into winter, increasingly all I needed in my life was Bilbo. Once he came along I spent less time out partying and more time with him. I did everything for him; I would hardly think of myself, always considering him first. As far as I was concerned, we'd made a commitment to each other. I noticed early on that Bilbo would always lie in the doorway. That way, I couldn't go anywhere without him knowing. And as soon as I moved he'd be up, because he didn't want to be left on his own. I had promised him I would never leave him on his own again, and I didn't.

Even if we were at a function or talk and I had to leave the room to go for a toilet break or to fetch something from the car, I would ask someone to hold him for me. When I returned they'd always say: 'Do you know what? He hasn't taken his eyes off that door.' And if anybody got in the way he'd be craning his neck around them, so he could always keep sight of the door.

Just after I got him we were checking one of the buoyancy aids at a beautiful spot called Logan Rock on the south coast near the Minack Theatre. It was quite a long walk down from the car park through the fields and Bilbo really liked it. Because I had to scramble round the cliff to reach the buoyancy aid and it wasn't safe for Bilbo, I tied him to a rock with a long piece of rope. But, like I say, Bilbo didn't want to let me out of his sight and once he got a head of steam up the power in him was phenomenal.

He looked at me anxiously, as if to say, 'Where are you going?!' I asked him to 'stay' and 'wait!' and clambered off over the rocky outcrop, out of sight. It took me a couple of minutes to reach the buoyancy aid and, as I was checking it, I became aware of a presence. I turned around and there he was, as pleased as punch, right there beside me. He'd snapped the rope in the middle, and it was as thick as a man's finger. That's how strong he was.

Back at Chez Noir he loved sleeping in the kitchen, where I made up a bed for him with a lambswool blanket. They say dogs don't sweat but the blanket would be damp in the morning and I never understood why until a good friend bought him a proper dog bed, which was quite expensive but didn't get damp because it let the air circulate freely. He loved that bed.

Billy used to wake me up at the same time every morning – about half six – and we would have a fuss together. Because my place was often cold in the mornings, I used to sit next to him with a blanket over the both of us. We'd sit there and get ready to go out for the day. We kept to our little daily routine. I'd have a cup of tea and then open the door and step out onto the cliff path to go for our morning walk. When we got back I would make him some scrambled eggs for breakfast and then get his brushes and combs and spend about an hour grooming him. He loved being groomed. I used to talk to him the whole time I was brushing him. I would tell him he was 'my boy' and that I would never leave him.

That done, we'd head down to the lifeguard hut and to work, Bilbo trotting ahead of me with his tail up and ears pricked, both of us happy as Larry.

It was bliss. The sun was shining, I had my faithful dog at my side and the prospect of a day at the most beautiful office in the world ahead of me. It was our own little kingdom and I counted myself very fortunate indeed.

6

Rules Are Meant to Be Broken

There was, however, a potential fly in the ointment vis-à-vis my plan to have Bilbo with me at work. For while Gwynver beach was dog friendly, our canine chums were not allowed on the beach at Sennen during the summer months.

It was decided quite early on, though, that since it was already abundantly obvious that Bilbo wasn't just any old dog, the rules wouldn't apply to him. And, after all, I had told my boss, quite plainly, that I was only prepared to take Bilbo on if I could bring him to work with me every day. And as I worked on the beach, it was a given that Bilbo would be allowed on it too.

'Yep, that's fine,' he said. 'But how are we going to get around the ban?' Initially I'd thought Bilbo could just stay up at the hut. But he was very gregarious and because of his size and character the kids on the beach noticed him and immediately took to him. For his part, he clearly enjoyed interacting with the youngsters and I had the thought that he could be the best tool for teaching beach safety that we had ever had.

Newfoundlands are naturally adapted to swimming in water, especially the harsh cold water of the Labrador Current in Canada, where they hail from. They have a double coat, the top layer of which is waterproof and keeps the fine-haired coat underneath dry and warm even in the sea – their own wetsuit, essentially. When they swim, their ears stick flat to the sides of their head, like large flaps, which prevents water from getting into their ears. Their long legs give them plenty of power to move through the water and the webs between their toes are bigger than on other breeds and work like massive paddles to propel them along. They also have extra-large lungs, which give them lots of endurance, while their big tails act as a rudder when they're swimming.

Bilbo was so excited by going into the sea – or any water actually. Whenever an alert came in I soon noticed that his ears would start twitching. He was very perceptive and always knew when something was on. I realized quite quickly that we could use Bilbo on the beach and put his natural love of water to good use. The germ of an idea started to grow that if I could get a red and yellow coat made for Bilbo (red and yellow being the colours of the flags on the beach where it is safe to bathe), children in particular would almost certainly get the message.

I mentioned the idea to Martin, the manager at the Old Success Inn, which is right beside the beach at Sennen and was my and Bilbo's local, and he offered to pay for the jacket to be made. I designed it myself out of a lightweight, breathable material so he wouldn't get too hot on summer days and soon Bilbo was the proud owner of his very own lifeguard jacket in the bright red and yellow lifeguard colours, with the message 'Swim Between the Flags' printed on the side. As I strapped Bilbo in, he looked at me inquisitively, not quite sure what was going on. But after a couple of sniffs, he soon came round. In fact, he seemed to like wearing it and looked rather fetching in his new uniform, even if I do say so myself. Rather like a caped crusader! His attitude changed when he had his jacket on. He would be 'on parade'. A bit like a racehorse going to a race, he pranced and looked around. Bilbo *loved* attention.

I figured that if we put him on our quad bike he wouldn't actually be on the beach because he'd be sitting on the quad. It was left to me to square it with the council. I said to them, 'Listen, we can actually use him on the beach but we won't put him *on* the beach as such. Once he's in the water then it's a different story. How about that?'

They thought long and hard. 'Mmm, well all right then,' was the reply. They understood what I was talking about and could see that having a lifeguard dog could be a great thing for Cornish tourism and a great thing to promote lifeguarding. And, sure enough, it didn't take long for news of our latest employee to get out.

One of the local radio stations, Pirate FM, was doing an interview on the beach with Penwith Lifeguard Service prior to the season starting, and the interviewer asked my boss about the new signs that had just gone up, telling bathers where was safe to swim in a new, pictorial form.

'But haven't they cost thousands of pounds?' she asked him, her tone doubtful.

'You'd better ask Steve about that,' he said, neatly side-stepping her interrogation. I wasn't expecting to be interviewed and was momentarily thrown.

'Well?' the interviewer said, looking at me expectantly.

'The only thing I can tell you about signage,' I said, 'is that nobody pays a blind bit of notice to a sign. They hang their clothes on them, they walk straight past them; they're on holiday, they don't want to read signs or be told what to do. Hopefully these newly designed ones will attract more attention. However, with our new secret weapon . . .' and at this point I opened the door to my 4x4 and Bilbo jumped out. 'This is going to change the face of lifeguarding!'

'How's that?' she asked, breaking into a smile at the sight of Bilbo.

'I've got him a red and yellow coat to wear on the beach and that'll be our new sign,' I said. 'Not only that' – and at this point I surprised even myself – 'we're going to train him to actually rescue people!'

'Oh, great,' she said. 'We'll definitely have to come back and feature that.'

So Bilbo was allowed a special dispensation provided he stayed on the back of my quad bike and wore his life vest. I trained him to ride safely on the back of the quad while we crossed the beach, stopping at intervals so everyone could meet Bilbo and read the message on his coat. Soon the phrase was everywhere: 'Bilbo says swim between the flags.' A celebrity was born!

Bilbo would also sometimes ride out with us on the Rescue Ski that patrolled the deep water. He'd sit on the sled on the back, from where he could dive off to assist swimmers in trouble and tow them back to safety. And of course he *was* on the beach as well as on the quad but no one minded because he would always do his business at home.

Essentially he was the sixth member of our team of highly trained, capable lifeguards. And he soon brought international interest to Penwith Council. They were getting emails from all over the world – as far as America, Australia, Indonesia, South Africa – from people asking, 'Can you tell us more about your lifeguard dog?'

So it was an unspoken agreement that Bilbo worked for the council as part of our lifeguard team. He wasn't paid, although I used to put a time sheet in for him, just as a tongue-in-cheek thing. But then I used to get irate phone calls from the wages department: 'Stop putting these ridiculous time sheets in for Bilbo!'

We had to run the beach with an iron fist; it was the only way. I had learnt that during my years at Gwynver. Because if people found you wanting, they'd take advantage. To keep control of a beach with seven thousand people on it, you can't afford to have posing lifeguards who strut their stuff. Neither women nor guys want to be talked down to by some egotistical lifeguard – especially one who's wearing shades all the time. I wanted my guards to be polite but firm.

We had frequent run-ins with surfers on Sennen who did not want to be hemmed into the surfing area and chose instead to surf close to our bathing area. They were also starting to discard their leashes in favour of a more 'free style of surfing, man!' I could sort of understand their point of view but they never really got mine, and we were at loggerheads a lot. Before leashes were introduced, I'd seen it plenty of times; people would be surfing behind bathers and would lose their surfboard. They'd try and swim to it, but the next wave would come and take it further away from them and this thing would then go hurtling through the surf where people were swimming and could easily smash someone's head open. Or knock their teeth out. There were also children collecting shells in the shallows and they could potentially be hit too. Bathers would often complain to me about that.

Some of the guys were competent enough to hold on to their boards but they were setting an example to others to go surfing without a leash, while we were insisting, 'Look, if you're going to go and surf behind bathers you've got to have a leash on. Because if you lose your board it could crucify a child.' They were surfing on nine-foot surfboards – and although they are comparatively light, they are made of fibreglass and still weigh about seven kilos. They're hard, and if you get hit by one, you will know all about it. It happened every summer – we were patching up people's heads all the time. We all became really good at it!

There were many surfers who got hit by their own boards too. One girl was pushing her long board out by the tail and the wave took it and it hit her on the head. By the time we got her out of the water she couldn't feel her feet and we had to treat it as a suspected spinal injury, which can be an absolute nightmare for both casualty and lifeguard, especially if it is a flooding tide. And that's someone who was just pushing the board out, not surfing on it. Another time I saw this absolute buffoon in fancy dress come sliding in sideways on a massive windsurfing board with no leash on it and recognized him as my young friend and neighbour Lee, whose nickname is Leroy. 'Leroy, get out of the swimming area now, God damn you!' I shouted in my best head lifeguard voice.

'Chill out, man,' he replied. 'We're only having a contest.'

Well – that was it! 'I'll give you chill out in a minute, you
little tyke,' I screamed.

'But I'm a local,' he bleated.

'A local! I don't care if you're Captain Blinking Nemo,
get out of the area,' I yelled. But he knew what he'd been
doing was stupid and he apologized later.

The power of some waves can be fearsome. I've seen
people lose their clothes in the shore break and bikinis
disappear! The waves roll them around and then strip cos-
tumes completely off. I even witnessed an elderly person
break a leg, a compound fracture with bone showing
through the skin, just from the shore break – the momentum of the wave picking them up and slamming them into
the wet sand. Another guy, surfing the shore break, was
picked up and dumped by a wave and had the end of his
surfboard fin shoved up his bottom. Ouch! It went clean
through his wetsuit, because they can be quite sharp. He
was taken to hospital to be stitched up, poor chap.

Our lifeguard hut was high up on the dunes at a stra-
tegic vantage point and I realized quite early on that if
you're running a team of four or five people you want to
make sure that that team works perfectly throughout the
whole day. You don't want people getting bored or fed up
because they've been told to get down to the water's edge
and stay there until they're told to come up. When I first
started, a lot of senior guides would say, 'Right, he can stay
down there for a couple of hours while we have a cup of
rosy.' And they'd just leave them down there. In those days
we weren't issued with sunglasses and hours of staring into

glaring surf often resulted in headaches. The lifeguard would get tired and lose concentration and take his eye off the ball.

At Sennen we divided each day into half-hour sectors and at the end of that half-hour everybody would switch. You'd do half an hour on lookout at the hut – and it was only half an hour so there was no talking to girlfriends or anybody who comes up off the beach, you look at the beach and that's all you do. You've got a radio and a pair of binoculars and your job for thirty minutes is to watch that whole beach. You're looking for things like a group of people suddenly massing together. Why's that happening, could somebody be having a heart attack? Is there something going on down there? Get on your radio and ask a lifeguard to go and look at the situation.

You might see people walking down the beach with body boards without flippers, going towards the surfing area. If you haven't got flippers on you're a swimmer and you have less power to get away from those rips. With a pair of fins on you've got much more power, even if you're not a good swimmer. You're holding on to a body board and you've got enough propulsion to come away from those rips. So the rule is, you can go in the surfing area if you've got flippers on. But most people don't know that and if we let some people go in without flippers you've got to let everybody in without flippers because they'll just say, 'Well, what about him?'

The guy on lookout would be checking the whole beach and we'd have two lifeguards down at the water's edge, another on first aid duty at the hut, and one would be having half an hour off, just to have a cup of tea or get something to eat, or even have a quick surf. Then you'd go down onto the beach and that's when we'd do PR with the public and you weren't necessarily looking at the sea all the time because the guy on lookout was doing that.

We'd all have a call sign – mine was Zulu – that would be used for specific areas on the beach: Sennen One, Sennen Two etc. so the guy in the hut just needs to say, 'Sennen One, turn around, you've got two body boarders at four o'clock – direct them to the swimming area.'

It goes without saying that when you're working as a team you've got to have a conscientious crew that know the rules. For example, you can't afford to have guards who react too quickly and throw the binoculars down so that the next time someone picks them up the prisms have moved, one eye's gone out of focus and you could miss something. So you have to have people who are responsible working for you. The role of the lookout is crucial: forewarned is forearmed, I used to tell them.

Things happen so fast here. Our rips on these beaches around Land's End can be exceptionally strong and events can unfold rapidly, so observation is the key. Not only did we watch the beach but also all access points to the beach. That included the coast path where weary, hot walkers often clambered down amongst the rocks on the approach to the beach and before you knew it they could be heading for the surf as far as four hundred metres away. So lookout duty also included regular sweeps of the coast path. Sometimes you have to use a bit of common sense too, because there are people who just go into the sea to relieve themselves. As an inexperienced lifeguard you could easily shout at them to get out when all they want is to have a wee.

Especially ladies. Better to just observe, and if they look like they are about to start swimming, move in then.

I used to tell the lifeguards, 'I want you to be like the farmer who knows his work inside out. When he goes to look at his field of cattle he'll have a quick shufti around and he'll notice if something is wrong straight away. That's what I want you to be like. When you come to the beach I want you to seek out the anomalies – a group of people crowding around or somebody waving their arms in the air – things like that.'

Working together and socializing together we inevitably forged close bonds. But my lifeguards had to earn my respect, as I'm sure I did theirs. Janus Howard was a young surfer who came to work with me when he was nineteen. At the time I wondered what the heck Penwith's chief lifeguard and our 'illustrious leader' John Sager was thinking. I said to him: 'Why have you done this to me, John? You've given me this kid who's only worked one season on a beach and you've put him to work with me on *Gwynver*?'

Because Gwynver was a dangerous beach, make no mistake. It used to claim lives all the time before there was such a thing as lifeguards. Locals would never swim there – if you talk to anyone who is a true local here about swimming on Gwynver they'll all say their parents never allowed them to go down there because there was talk of quicksand.

But John just said, 'I've put him with you because I want you to teach him, that's why I've placed him there.'

I said, 'Well that's all very well, but this is a working beach. I'm teaching him *and* running the beach at the same time then?' I was a bit aggrieved because I thought I would be looking and working for the pair of us in the early days, but Janus came good and became a great lifeguard. We worked on Gwynver for ten years and we had a really good partnership in the end.

In poor weather when there was nobody on the beach for days on end the two of us used to sit and discuss 'What if . . .' What would happen if you found yourself down on the rocks and there was a massive sea running and there was somebody in trouble in front of you? What would you do? Would you go for the helicopter option or would you go in and try and save them yourself? We'd sit and mull this over for hours at a time. Land ambulances could take anything up to an hour to get to Sennen and there were only two or three in the west of the county anyway. In the summertime they would be pretty stretched and might even have to come from as far as forty miles away, so for serious first aid we would be thinking about tasking either the Cornwall Air Ambulance or RNAS Culdrose search and rescue helicopters with the job, as they could be on the scene within as little as twenty minutes.

And then one day it happened to me.

7

On the Rocks

It was the height of the season and there was a massive swell building. It was one of those summer swells that popped up out of nowhere – a one-day wonder. Sometimes in the summer a big intense low will form in the Atlantic and will just be there long enough to kick up a big swell, then it will dissipate but the swell will keep coming towards the shore. You might notice the night before as the tide's coming in that the swell is starting to get up and the next morning it could be huge. And it could be gone the next day. So it can come up, be massive, and then just vanish and be gone again because there's nothing more pushing it.

And that's what happened on a day in August 1993. The beach was packed and we had red flags out warning people not to swim because it was super dangerous – the swell hitting the beach was a good eight feet, I'd say. People measure waves from different perspectives. A lot of people measure from the bottom of the trough to the top – so as the wave rears up and is about to break they'll reckon from there to the trough as the height of the wave. But we don't; we measure from the back of the wave. So an eight-foot wave to us could possibly be seen as something like a fifteen-foot wave to others.

Anyway, there were big, big waves coming in and we were red-flagged right across Gwynver beach and even on Sennen. Although we were keeping all bathers out of the water that day, we'd had canoeists and surfers in the sea – and surfers are kind of a law unto themselves so we would look at each surfer and say to ourselves: 'Has he got his wetsuit on the right way round? Yep. Is he carrying his board properly? Yep. Leash? Yes. Right, he probably knows what he's about.' So we'd allow them to go in. After all, Gwynver was and still is one of the best beach-breaks in the south-west and that's what a lot of these guys were here for. Then you'd see others walking down the beach with the zip down the front of their wetsuit, so they've got it on back to front for starters, and they most definitely shouldn't be allowed in.

It was about four o'clock in the afternoon when it happened. The tide was pushing in and it was nearly high tide so it was all up on the rocks. I was on duty on Gwynver beach and had seen two body boarders come over from Sennen, but the waves were just too big and they couldn't really handle it. You have to have shape in a wave and sometimes when the waves come that quickly the rips are fluctuating and strong, and the waves are all over the place with no shape. And it was like that on that day.

Somebody said, 'There's a guy in trouble over there between Sennen and Gwynver,' so I radioed Janus, grabbed a pair of fins and a Peterson tube and ran over. One of the guys had lost his board and he was trying to swim in to the beach but the tide was pushing and waves were now breaking directly onto the rocks. His pal was already paddling back to Sennen. Potentially we had full short-wave radio communications, but budgets were tight and battery packs, being old, often went down after prolonged use. That was what happened to mine on that day. I had however already radioed Janus and told him to await my call and keep a sharp lookout.

The set waves were coming every six minutes or so – and six minutes is quite a long time. I thought: I can make it out there. But when I went and had a look where he was I just thought: This could be a recipe for disaster. I was standing on the rocks with a Peterson tube, which is a type of buoyancy aid, and a pair of flippers, not thinking that I was going to have to go in the water. But I realized that if he got caught in all that surf the guy was going to end up being thrown on the rocks, which would have mashed him to pieces.

I thought: What am I going to do? And reckoned a helicopter was probably the best option. But in the time it would take for the helicopter to arrive, would he have hit the rocks? At this point I looked round and there were about fifty people standing on the cliff path right behind me and my heart just sank. I said to myself, 'What are you going to do now? You're the head lifeguard on this beach; are you going to do something or are you going to walk back to the hut, pick your bags up and clear off?' Because my credibility would have gone straight out the window if I didn't do something.

But at the same time I knew it wasn't safe for me to go in.

Standing on the rocks, my legs were like jelly as I thought, How am I going to get out of this one? I knew it was only fifty-fifty whether I'd make it or not. But then I realized that when the big sets came through and broke on the rocks and sucked back, you couldn't see any rocks. And I reckoned that if I dived in on the back of a big wave that hit the rocks it would then suck me clear and I'd be in the area where the waves were starting to break. Then it would just be a matter of trying my hardest to swim out through them to where the guy was. That was the idea anyway.

I screamed at him, 'Go back! Turn round!' Because I wanted him to swim out to sea, away from the break. It was no good. I realized I just had to go for it, so I waited for the last wave of the set and dived in on the back of this wave into the maelstrom. Water was breaking everywhere. Thank God Bilbo wasn't with me in those days because I think he would have followed me in and in those conditions even he might have drowned. I was trying to power through the waves but I could feel the Peterson tube pulling me back. I was swimming and swimming and finding it difficult to get a breath in the foaming surf. I was shouting to the guy to turn round – and he'd lost a flipper now too. Thank God he did; he started to swim back out.

And then I saw this wave doing what we call 'feathering' – it was just getting bigger and bigger and then the wind starts to blow the wave back and you get this big plume come up off the wave. And I saw the guy just scratch over the top of that wave and I knew then he was far enough out that he wouldn't get caught up in it.

However, I was still looking at this massive thing that was now coming at me. I dived underneath it but the Peterson tube pulled me back again and I was getting more and more tired. And the next thing, I just looked down and there was something black by me and it was a rock. I'd been pushed back in onto the rocks now myself.

Meanwhile, back on Gwynver, Janus was keeping watch on the beach from the hut, unable to see where I was but beginning to get the picture that my radio might have gone down, when he spotted a good friend of ours, Harvey, waving and running up the beach.

Janus had recently been to Mundaka, down in Spain, surfing some monstrous waves, and he'd perfected this technique called duck-diving, which we hadn't heard much about at the time. As the wave rears up and you're paddling out on your board, if you push the front of the board down just as the wave is about to break over you and press with a foot or knee on the back of the board you'll come out the back of the wave, effectively passing clean through it.

Harvey had seen me dive off the rocks from the beach and Janus knew that I was going to have a lot of trouble with the waves. He could now see that the guy was swimming out to sea and he told me afterwards that he nearly died himself that day trying to reach him. He did a fantastic job, and it took him ages, but Janus got to the guy and he took him all the way back to Sennen beach. He was a real hero.

Whereas I was stuck on these rocks now, trying to think what I'm going to do next, and the waves are sucking back and what had seemed a little black thing became a massive rock. I could see the next set of waves coming in so I grabbed on to this rock as tight as I could and just held on for dear life.

And then – *boom!* It hit the rock and I was sent up in the air, and all I could do was just put my hands out in an attempt to brace myself as it smashed me into the rock. My mouth took the full impact and I felt my front teeth push backwards – and I had really nice teeth too. My neck was wrenched back too by the force and I had a mouthful of blood. I was just lucky it hadn't hit me on the top of the head because if it had knocked me out I could easily have drowned. The power of the waves was absolutely incredible; I'd seen them move massive rocks overnight, but never actually felt that force until then.

Bystanders had knotted towels together and came down onto the rocks and threw the towelling rope to me, and I managed to scramble up it and out of the water as the next waves were hitting me. I had escaped – but I was covered in blood and my arms and legs were shredded. Janus told me afterwards that I was lucky to be alive.

Some people helped me to the hut and there were enough surfers around to take care of me. In those days there wasn't any such thing as health and safety and people didn't make a fuss, so we didn't call an ambulance or anything. I just drove myself to hospital later that day.

An emergency dentist looked at my mouth and gave me some injections. He took out my two front teeth and I had to go back in the next day and have an operation. That was even worse than the accident because they stuffed cotton wool down my throat and then they lanced the top of my gum. It was horrendous. They told me I couldn't have implants because the bone had been fractured, so now I have a plate that I've got to put up with, which is a real pain, but that's the way it is. It has changed the shape of my face slightly, but I'm lucky I don't look like a horse! I've seen a lot of people who look like they've got a face full of wooden teeth when they have false ones, but at least mine sort of look all right.

Because I had a red flag flying it was really too dangerous and I should never have gone into the water. But that's the way it happened. I was caught between the devil and the deep blue sea. I knew that day that it was a huge risk – it was obvious because the swell was so massive. And I knew that it was about evens whether I'd make it out alive.

Suffice to say, I never doubted Janus after that. And that was why it always riled me when people saw us lifeguards as poseurs and thought that Bilbo was just for show. It was all about saving lives.

8

Two Men and a Dog

In the mid-eighties I took a break from lifeguarding for a few years to go fishing out of Cape Cornwall, which has the distinction of being the only cape in England. I wanted to learn how the tides worked down here – a key part of my education in becoming a waterman. The local fishermen are highly protective of 'their' patch and don't often share with strangers but I was very privileged to be allowed to become part of the Cape Cornwall Slipway Association. One of the reasons they allowed me was because I was a Shetlander, not English – the next best thing to being Cornish! Even so, I had to work hard to earn my place, spending a year working 'in the bow' with an old hand before I was allowed to have my own boat. It was hard graft. We were double tripping, which means we were going to sea twice a day. We'd muster at about half past three in the morning to launch and go up the coast in the dark. It was fantastic!

We'd go up to Pendeen lighthouse and fish the tide up there, pulling a few lobster pots on the way back. We'd get back at about ten o'clock, land our fish, get the boats pulled up, put our engines away, load our fish in the van and take it to Newlyn. We'd get it on the market, come back, go to bed, get up at three in the afternoon, go back down to the cove and go out again at about four o'clock in the afternoon and fish until about nine at night. Then we would come back and repeat the whole procedure. And we'd do that for two months solid. You can only get away from there in the summertime because the seas are too rough in the winter.

Reminiscing years later down at the Cape with Bilbo, I told him all about it. 'You would have come with me, Bill, we would have looked after each other and you would have enjoyed all that fresh fish,' I said, as we watched the fishing boats heading out to sea. They were happy days indeed.

Anyway, I digress. Back on Sennen I took charge of a new team and enlisted a lifeguard called Mark as my second in charge. We became good friends – not least because he would later love Bilbo almost as much as I did.

Mark was – in his own words – 'a bit of a rebel' when he first came to lifeguarding. A Penzance boy, he was a keen surfer and considered Sennen his home patch. Over the years he had watched as many had tried and failed to join the ranks of those who guarded the beaches around Land's End.

Myself and Lloyd, as unofficial supervisors, were in charge of lifeguard selection and induction at the time and I had watched Mark's progress over a couple of years. The more I thought about a team selection for Sennen and Gwynver, the more Mark stood out as a potential second in command. He was sufficiently feisty for the job, certainly fit and able enough, and someone who I believed could be moulded into a first-class surf lifeguard. In selecting Mark to second the team, however, I realized I would have to keep him in check and not let it go to his head. So, on one of his first days working on Sennen, I took him down to the water's edge – as I did with each new lifeguard – and had a quiet word with him. 'Look, you have been chosen as a Sennen lifeguard which is quite an achievement in itself,' I said. 'However, now you have to realize that it also means you are a Sennen lifeguard not only *in* work but *out* of work as well.'

I could tell he wasn't really sure what I meant and so I explained. 'If something kicks off and we are not officially at work, we all still look after one another. We cover our backs.' I could see Mark thinking, 'What have I signed up for?'

We met when he was eighteen and now, two years on, we were working together. Despite the age gap between us we became good friends. I suppose I was a bit of a father figure to him, in that he was a similar age to my son and told me his dad hadn't been around when he was a kid. Because I had experienced a family break-up myself I was very aware of the impact it had on our children and was perhaps a bit more receptive to Mark than the other life-guards might have been. I could see that some of the guys at the depot thought Mark rather pedantic, but then I was thinking, 'Yep, I can use that!'

But I also believed in the team and that is what I tried to drum into Mark. 'No one in this team wants to hear you whinge. You have to think of all of us here,' I told him. 'We are all stronger if we are one.' And I could tell he had respect for that. Although I was older than the others, we never discussed age. It never seemed to matter; in their eyes I was out partying as hard as they were. I would be out most nights during the summer, making the most of the beach lifestyle.

I'd like to think I was friendly to the youngsters, but only just enough to keep them in line. Like I said, Mark and I hit it off straight away although it took him a couple of years to calm down. On quiet days when the beach was deserted we would just sit and talk. 'You don't need to prove yourself, just roll with it,' I'd say. But he confided in me later on that because he grew up without a dad, he always felt there was something missing and that he did have to prove himself. 'I was just fighting life a little bit,' he admitted.

And while I didn't realize at the time that I was the only male who had ever bothered to coach him, I was fond of Mark and occasionally worried what might become of him if he didn't calm down.

Things came to a head one evening when he crashed his bike doing motocross without the proper gear on. He broke his foot in thirteen places and was told he'd never walk again. I remember going to see him in the hospital and telling him how silly he was. In the event, he was lucky because he did walk again. But he had to spend six months in a wheelchair and endure some pretty serious operations and intensive physiotherapy. I visited him while he was recuperating and I'd wheel him down to the lifeguard hut and tell him stories. And eventually he realized he could be doing better things with his time than hurting himself.

I think Bilbo later helped Mark find his way in life too. Shortly before I adopted Bilbo, Mark and I spent the

weekend working on the beach and I told him I was thinking of taking him on and was planning on bringing him to
work with me. Mark immediately said, 'Well, I will help
you out. I'll help you look after him.' He soon came to love
Bilbo and the three of us quickly became The Team.

Bilbo had been on the beach with us in an unofficial
capacity in 2005 but in 2006 he came to work on Sennen
properly, becoming Britain's first – and only – active surf
lifeguard dog. In fact I believe he was the world's first fully
qualified surf lifeguard dog. Qualified in that he could
match the swim times and response criteria required of us
human lifeguards, that is. After our local radio station
Pirate FM ran the feature about Bilbo, it planted the seed.
A news agency picked the story up and it ended up in the
national press.

The *Sun* newspaper came down and did a photo-shoot
with Bilbo on the beach. Everyone was looking really cool
in the article – Bilbo included. The day it came out, the
phone was literally ringing off the hook in the lifeguard hut.
I answered it for what felt like the hundredth time that
morning and it was our local BBC TV news programme,
Spotlight.

Afterwards, I hung up the phone, sucked my teeth,
looked at Mark and said, 'We're stuffed, my boy.'

'Why's that?' he asked.

'Because they only want to come and film Bilbo actually
doing a rescue!' I replied gravely. 'Hmmm . . .'

To be fair, rescuing people wasn't Bilbo's job. It was
ours. While he was a valued member of the team, he hadn't
been involved in any actual rescues at this point. His job, as
I saw it, was public relations and promoting beach safety.

Plus, it would hardly have been responsible to put a dog in the position of looking after thousands of people's safety. Initially he was just a mascot for Sennen lifeguard service. I had, however, made that reckless remark that I was going to train him to save people and now I would have to put my money where my mouth was.

'Well,' said Mark. 'He swims out to me when I'm surfing – how long have we got?'

'They're coming the week after next,' I said. 'So come on – we'd better get started.'

9

Bilbo Earns His Stripes

I knew that Bilbo had it in him to become a fully fledged lifeguard dog because of precedent in his breed. Newfoundlands are incredibly strong and can easily tow three men at once, or even a boat into harbour. Because they were such good swimmers, the fishermen in Newfoundland used them to swim the ropes back to the shore from the nets. This was before the Victorian era, before they had steam capstans and machines like that. In those days the men would have to haul the ropes themselves and would have to row the ropes ashore. The fishermen noticed that not only could these dogs survive in the really cold water – there was an instance of one swimming around in the Atlantic for five days before being picked up by a boat – they were strong enough to pull ropes. If a man fell in the water the dog would jump in and swim over to him and pull him back to shore. They were never taught to do that; it was just an instinctive thing in that breed of dog.

So the fishermen trained the Newfoundlands to take a rope and swim it to shore. They were also used to transport the fish to market, pulling dog carts through the narrow streets that were too small for a horse and cart. In the late eighteenth century and 1800s, because of their renown in the maritime world they became popular as 'ship dogs', due to their good, 'caring' nature, apparent ability to exist without much exercise, plus an extraordinary instinct to rescue people. And because they could rescue, seamen would take them whaling as well. When they arrived at the whaling ground the men would release a number of smaller boats and they'd row around trying to find the whales to stick their harpoons into them. And of course the whales didn't like that and they would take umbrage and thrash around and sometimes the little boats would get smashed up.

The dogs would be on the mother ship and when the little port or starboard doors were opened for them they would swim out and rescue the men in the water. The Newfoundland is documented as having saved lots of lives. If you are knocked out by an oar or something, you usually end up face down in the water – there are not many unconscious people who end up floating on their backs, for some reason. But because the dogs would grab the drowning men by the arm as they turned to swim them back, it would have the effect of turning the casualties onto their backs, trawling their bodies, which opened their airways and they survived.

Years ago there were also instances where boats were shipwrecked and no one could get a line ashore. Someone would have to swim it to shore and often they would drown. Or they'd tie a rope to a volunteer who'd get dashed to pieces on the rocks. There are loads of accounts where Newfoundlands have taken the rope, swum it to shore and saved the whole ship's company, which on a passenger ship could be as many as two hundred.

When we began training Bilbo, Mark and I took him down to the far end of Sennen beach, where it was quieter, and to start with I would swim out and Mark would stay with Bilbo on the beach. He'd then let him go and Bilbo would swim out to me. But then of course he wouldn't swim back in because he wanted to be with me. He just started mucking around trying to grab me, so I decided the only way to do it was for Mark to go out first, and then Bilbo could swim out to him and back to me.

Bilbo didn't know what to do to start with – but then again, neither did we! He would swim out to Mark all right, but he kept swimming into him, ripping his wetsuit with his sharp claws. When we looked at our wetsuits after the first few training sessions they were full of little dings and holes from Bilbo's teeth and claws. The wetsuits were supplied by different sponsors every season and were quite precious to the lifeguards. You had to look after them and give them back in reasonable condition. Mark managed to get Bilbo to stop swimming into him by splashing water in his face – because Bilbo didn't like water in his eyes – and that's how he trained him to swim around us.

As well as his lifeguard coat, Bilbo would wear a special harness onto which we clipped a Peterson tube, the piece of equipment used by all lifeguards to rescue casualties. If someone fears they are in danger of drowning they can panic and just grab hold of the person trying to rescue them. If you are not careful they can end up dragging you down beneath the water with them – and this could easily have happened to Bilbo too so we had to train him not to swim too close to the person in trouble. By using the Peterson tube there were two metres of line between Bilbo and the casualty, which would prevent them from trying to climb on top of him. We taught Bilbo to swim close to Mark, and swim around him in a circle until he caught hold of the Peterson tube. Eventually, once Bilbo felt Mark's weight clutching the tube, he knew it was time to turn round and swim back to the beach, towing Mark safely in behind him.

There are groups of people who put on displays of Newfoundlands, who will tow boats and rescue people out at sea, but Bilbo is the only one I've ever heard of who has been trained to use a Peterson tube like a surf lifeguard. And the Peterson tube is the secret to the whole success of it, because without that people would have grabbed Bilbo himself. It's human instinct. One of the first things you're taught when you become a lifeguard is how to evade people's clutches, because they will try to latch on to you. If somebody is drowning they will grab you so hard you've got to know what you're doing to get away from them. You use pressure points, as in a martial art like ju-jitsu. So if they clasp your arm, you just work against their thumbs and they will let go.

If people try to grab you around the head you have to deal with them in a very firm manner – although we'd concentrate on their body rather than smack them in the mouth – and climb down their body until you're under the water. Then they will let you go because nobody who is in fear of drowning wants to go under the water.

Sometimes you get two swimmers who are locked together and are so terrified they won't let each other go.

They just clutch each other in a grip and it's difficult to get them apart, so we employ a technique of using our feet to separate them.

So once Mark took hold of the Peterson tube I would call Bilbo in. He actually got the idea pretty quickly. To start with Mark swam along with Bilbo, only gradually putting a bit of weight on the tube and then his full weight. Bilbo zigzagged a little bit the first time he felt the weight on the tube, rather than swimming straight back in. But I kept shouting to him when he went off course and once he got used to it he didn't mind it.

I used the special whistle I'd had for him when I played hide and seek with him when he was a puppy. He was trained to look for the signal to come back, so he would do it on hand signals as well. He was trained in the same way as a lifeguard at sea: one hand in the air means return to the beach. There are other hand signals: two hands in the air means go further out to sea; both arms held horizontally means stay where you are. They are the internationally recognized signs but Bilbo was only taught the signal to come in because there was no point teaching him the others.

We did it by treat training him. He didn't get a treat when he swam out to Mark, obviously; only when he turned round and swam back to the beach would he get praise and a tasty biscuit or piece of chicken. It didn't take very long before he got the hang of it and within one week if someone was waving their arm and shouting, Bilbo would respond. Mind you, sometimes he was a bit too keen for his own good! Like the occasion we were at Porthchapel, an unmanned beach near Land's End, checking the buoyancy equipment. There was a group of young body boarders larking about and enjoying the waves and Bilbo heard them shrieking and splashing about. The next thing he was hoofing it across the beach into the sea and swimming straight out to these guys. They realized who he was and allowed him to tow them in to shore, hanging on to his tail. Luckily on that occasion they weren't in any danger and were just enjoying themselves, but Bilbo was there in case they needed him.

Within one week the rescue was perfected, certainly enough for the first TV show. Also, bear in mind we didn't have all day to train him because we had other duties. We were lifeguarding. It's not like we did hours and hours of training. *Spotlight* came down and it was really funny because they did all this filming on the land first, with us wondering if Bilbo would perform when his turn came. Mark admitted afterwards that he'd been really worried in case Bilbo just swam off.

Before Mark went into the water and swam out to where he would stop and wave his arm in the air, I gave him a look, as if to say, 'Here we go . . .' But Bilbo just nailed it. He did the actual rescue in one take, which was really good for us, and Bilbo was judged to have what it took to be a lifeguard: brains, brawn and killer good looks! After that we never had any problem getting Bilbo to perform for the cameras. And lots of people came down to film us, including *Animal Planet* and a German television company.

Mark used to run with Bilbo in the water beforehand to tire him out a little bit and once he'd done that he would be switched on for filming and would sit and do it all on command. It did make us laugh because on a few occasions we were filmed, you can see Mark sprinting up and down trying not to be the recipient of Bilbo's excited little bites and nips. As it was there were bite marks all down one arm of his wetsuit, the left side. I was covered in little bite marks too. At one point I had been considering having a tattoo of Billy on my arm but thankfully I regained my senses in time, realizing 'why bother?' because he had given me his own one anyway!

We also trained Bilbo to ride on the jet ski – not that he needed much in the way of training because he proved a natural. On his first ever go, he just jumped on the back of the ski, I drove out, Mark jumped off and waved and Bilbo leapt in and got him. He wasn't fazed at all.

The Newfoundland breed may be known for its instinctive lifesaving water-rescue skills but Bilbo still had to be put through some special swimming and fitness tests just like all the other human lifeguards. He learnt to swim in all types of sea conditions, negotiate the different surf, and swim out beyond the breaking waves. The thing that did take a bit of time, though, was encouraging him to swim through big waves. In the summertime it wasn't too bad because the waves are not usually that big and we could always get him to a part of the beach where there was not so much swell. We'd take him to the sheltered end, towards the harbour.

As a lifeguard, I was expected to be water fit, and to keep in shape in the summer Bilbo and I would swim together most mornings. We'd head out from the beach in front of the car park, swim around the lifeboat, which was moored up outside the harbour while they were building a new slipway, and then back in front of all the people who were sitting on the beach so they could see Bilbo swimming. That was probably about a mile and it would take us about fifty minutes.

But it could frequently take us just as long as that to get from the car park to the beach – and it was only a matter of yards – in the first place, because Bilbo was so popular with the public. We were stopped countless times walking across the car park by people asking, 'Oh, can we have a picture with Bilbo? Can we stroke him?' I always said that if I could have had a pound for every photograph taken I would have made a fortune because there were thousands.

When we eventually got to the beach I let him go and he'd run into the sea and wait for me. He'd never swim off on his own; he would just get in there and wait. Then I'd wade out and we'd start diving through these little waves. And Bilbo could even take on the head-high waves. He was a very strong dog so when he launched himself into them he could just torpedo through them. And because he had these big flap ears, they'd stick to his head and the water didn't go inside.

And he was smart, because quite often conditions could be challenging. One day at the end of a swim as we were returning to shore, we had to swim through, and slightly against, a small but stronger than normal rip current. Now usually, we would advise people who find themselves in a rip not to swim *against* the current but to swim *towards* where the waves are breaking or parallel to the shore. I was just thinking to myself that we could incorporate the rip in our training session, but when I turned round and looked for Bilbo he had had enough! He had swum to the side and out of the rip just as we had told everyone to do! There he was, standing on the rocks and looking at me as if to say, 'What are you doing out there, you fool?'

Bilbo became a local celebrity, and as any rock star will tell you, fame has its costs. Bilbo was no exception, and two years after he first came to the beach, he had his first diva moment. We were trying to go for a swim and Bilbo was getting frustrated because he didn't want to sit and have his photograph taken – he wanted to get in the sea. He was getting more and more agitated and I couldn't hold him. He was just leaping up and letting out these howls of impatience. So I said to the holidaymakers, 'Look, I'm going to have to take him to the sea, can you get your photographs when we come out because he'll have calmed down by then.'

I took him down the slipway onto the sand and we started walking across the beach. I thought I could let him off. He had his Peterson tube attached to him, which was dragging behind him, so I thought I could always catch on to that. But he was so excited he grabbed me on the arm with his teeth. He got hold of my wetsuit, lancing it open, and blood was instantly pouring down my arm.

Normally I would have given him a right smack around the chops for something like that, but there were a whole lot of people standing behind us and all they would have seen was me clouting him round the head, so I couldn't. So we just went for a swim. We were probably swimming for three-quarters of an hour and when we came out I'd forgotten about it because it was cold and I couldn't feel the pain. I was just walking out of the water with Bilbo when this little girl said to me, 'What's happened to your arm, mister, has he bitten you?'

It was just high spirits; he had no aggression to humans

in him whatsoever. At the lifeguard hut children would be massed around him, some even lying on top of him. Their parents would engage me in conversation, so I wouldn't really notice what Bilbo was doing. I looked down one day and there was this kid with a piece of marram grass, which is long sticky beach grass, a bit like a straw, and he was putting it inside Bilbo's nose. It must have been very irritating but Bilbo just sat there putting up with this and every now and then sticking his tongue out to lick his nose.

Friday was one of our favourite days of the week because the local fish and chip shop used to give all the lifeguards – Bilbo included – a free lunch. Bilbo just loved fish and he would have the fried fish, in batter, as a treat. He earned it from all the exercise he did when he was on the beach. He got to know the routine well and would often ride over with us on the quad to collect the fish and chips, receiving lots of attention along the way. Not to mention the many sausages he would charm from the shop's customers too! But Billy had good manners and would wait patiently until all the lifeguards had received theirs before his would be served up in his own, clean bowl. No chips, however, that was a rule. He would inevitably finish his before anyone else, and before we knew it there would be a shuffling and feet-stamping routine going on. 'More please!' And of course there were always scraps . . . and probably a chip or two, if I knew the lads!

But one week he obviously couldn't wait for Friday and he escaped from the lifeguard hut. It was a good half-mile to the chippy and he had to cross the road from the beach to get there, so he was quite lucky not to have got hit by a car.

We didn't know where he'd got to but, next thing, the phone rang. It was the chip shop asking us if we would like to go over and collect him. Mark jumped on the quad bike, drove over and whistled, and Bilbo came running out of the chip shop, jumped on the bike and executed a quick getaway! Mark said later that he didn't want to hang around over there to find out whose food Bilbo might have eaten. But Bilbo was one of the team and we look after our own.

10

Bilbo Goes to School

Traditionally, we lifeguards were invited to local schools just before the summer holiday season began to give the children a talk about beach safety. I had been doing it with Lloyd since 2000 but when I got Bilbo I realized what an asset he could be and suggested to Penwith Council that he could accompany us.

The council agreed, with the proviso that everything had to be done properly. I took out third-party public liability insurance for Bilbo, in case he accidentally knocked a child over or something. Fully grown by now and two years old, he was a lot bigger than most of the kids – he towered over them. I got the maximum amount of cover – three million pounds – which, given his size, was very expensive.

So Bilbo the lifeguard dog and his Captain (me) were cleared to visit schools. I'll never forget the first time we went to meet the kids. Before we left, I sat down and told him: 'Billy, what an opportunity we have here, my lad. Your mission begins. Together, we can spread the word, not just to the children but also to the teachers.' I then asked him if he was 'ready' and he screwed his head from side to side, ears all pricked up inquisitively.

When I had taken him with me as a pup, we always had time to talk to people, let them have a fuss with Bilbo and the obligatory photograph. So when it came to taking him into school to meet children, I had no reservations – other than keeping a keen eye on his potential clumsiness. After all, he was still quite puppy-like and a bit floppy – and I did not want him smothering a 'Year One' by mistake!

'Right, Billy,' I said as we were about to set off. 'Best behaviour today, please – Bilbo, be a *good boy*. If Bilbo is a *good boy* he can have one of *these* – YES?' I added, holding up one of his favourite treats. 'OK, my kiss, please.' I waited until he licked my face before I gave it to him, then I fired up the 4x4 and we headed off to work.

When we arrived with Bilbo in the back of the vehicle, it was like Father Christmas was visiting. The kids were in a frenzy by the time we got into the playground. They were crowding round as I was trying to unload him and I had to say, 'No, keep back,' because they all wanted to hug him.

I had time to quickly brush him down and put on his lifesaving coat – a routine he got to know and love – before setting ourselves up in either the gymnasium or a classroom, depending on the size of the school. This day it was two classes of pupils in one fairly large classroom. We had our box of props, plus towels, water bowl and treats as well as souvenirs for the children. There was no shortage of helpers offering to carry Bilbo's box in from the car.

We were ushered in to where about fifty children were sitting quietly and took up a place on the floor in front of them. You could have heard a pin drop. Bilbo and I made a point of sitting on the floor with them, down on their level, and we began.

'Hello, everybody, and thank you all for being so quiet for Bilbo,' I said. At this point Bilbo flopped down with a great theatrical sigh. I felt it important for the children to see Bilbo as primarily their friend who was here to help keep them and their pals safe when they went to the beach during their holidays. I took a fairly relaxed and peaceful approach to the lesson and it was an instant success.

Word soon spread throughout the school that *Bilbo* was here and lots of teachers and even the dinner ladies came in to listen to our talk, at the end of which Bilbo performed a couple of tricks and brought the house down! The instant feedback was sensational, with many commenting on how their 'eyes had been opened' to beach safety. We had been booked in initially for an hour, but it was almost two hours later when we left!

Loading Bilbo back into the 4x4, he was full of beans, pulling on my sleeve and looking into my eyes, as if to say: 'How did I do, Capt? How did I do? Me, Me, Me!'

We drove away, smiling children lining the playground in the warm spring sunshine still shouting his name. A very successful first school talk and the start of many to come.

Our beach safety talks evolved as we did them. Right from the beginning, even in those very early days, I realized Bilbo's potential. His relaxing demeanour oozed calm when he met people and I could tell he was unique. He possessed that *je ne sais quoi*, but without an ounce of conceit, and I could see how he captivated children and adults alike. Even people who admitted having no particular love for dogs found Bilbo intriguing. It was becoming obvious that, as a learning tool, there was no equal. And what he was doing was vitally important. Every year we hear reports of people drowning in and around our shores. Most of these incidents occur as a result of a lack of knowledge of the potential hazards of water.

Then Bilbo stepped into the ring! Very soon, we were in great demand. We were doing on average three or four a week – and sometimes two a day. There wasn't a single school that refused to let Bilbo visit. But then everyone made exceptions for Bilbo. For example, when it was the Newlyn Fish Festival – and no dogs are allowed on the harbour at any time – they let him in every year. Rules got waived for him. It was the same at the Sailing Club. Animals aren't allowed inside because food is served there, but Bilbo was allowed to come in.

I'd tailor our schools education programme according to how old the children were. They were generally between five and ten years old but we also did Redruth Academy where there were pupils in their teens. The focus was the beach flag system, which is internationally recognized. I'd explain that while swimming in the sea and playing in the surf is great fun, the sea is a powerful force that can overwhelm even the strongest swimmer and most experienced surfer. I'd tell them how to raise the alarm and what to do if in difficulty, both in the sea and on the beach.

Depending on their age – because I didn't want to scare them – I let them know that at any moment the sea can change from being calm, to having a current that could sweep a person out to sea further than they want to go. I explained that this could be very frightening and dangerous and could even cause a person to drown, which was why it was so important for them always to swim between the red and yellow flags, like Bilbo said. And if they saw a red flag on the beach, not to go in the sea. With five- and six-year-old children you can't really explain *why* lifeguards put flags on beaches – you just tell them they're there and to look for certain things. With the older children you can start to explain why the lifeguard puts his flags where he does, and why the flags move – because they don't stay in the same place all day, every day. But I don't go into that with the youngsters because I think it's too much for them to absorb.

With the teenagers I learnt to explain it in a more hard-hitting way, because I knew they were going to be the ones who would be taking on the waves and venturing into the sea without their parents. In the past local people would have known where the dangerous beaches were, whereas these days the footpaths are better and people are more adventurous, and they turn up on more remote beaches that locals would avoid.

Children love to build sandcastles and dig holes in the sand – sometimes quite big holes that they like to play in. Often the children themselves do not dig the holes but come across abandoned ones. You don't hear much about it, but every year children die when the sand collapses on top of them and they suffocate. I told the schoolchildren how dangerous it is to dig on the beach, describing how the sand will form tunnels and walls while it's wet, but as it dries out it becomes prone to collapse. I demonstrated this by using Bilbo as a prop. He would usually lie slumped on the floor by my feet, chilled out as ever, but – make no mistake – he knew exactly what was required of him and always played along brilliantly.

I said, 'Bilbo has come along and he's found this hole. He didn't dig the hole, did he, but he's found it and has gone into it. But then he starts to bark, and remember what I said about the sand drying? I'll be the sand now and Bilbo's in the hole and all of a sudden the sand collapses!' At this point I would push down gently on Bilbo's chest and he would oblige by letting his breath out in an impressively theatrical groan. The kids sat completely transfixed, their eyes getting bigger and bigger with wonder. I'd say, 'If I keep my hands here, like the sand, Bilbo can't breathe in.' Whereupon the atmosphere in the classroom would change and the kids would exclaim, 'Take your hands off, you have to let him go!' And I'd say, 'Yes, I will let Bilbo go, but the sand will not.'

That's the sort of impact Bilbo had – he wasn't just sitting there in the classroom inanimate; he interacted with the kids. And he could certainly act when I needed him to. We would do a trick he had learnt as a puppy, where I'd get him to sit on the floor and tell him, 'Wait for it, wait for it,' and then I'd shout, 'Bang!' and he'd collapse on the floor as if he'd been shot. The kids loved it.

'How many of you are surfers, how many of you have got boogie boards?' Loads of them would put their hands up. And I'd tell them, 'Always make sure you've got your leash wrapped round your wrist properly and never, ever throw your body board away because it could save your life by keeping you afloat.' If inexperienced body boarders get into difficulty, the first thing most of them do is to throw it away and start swimming. Well, that's fatal, because now you're actually in the water instead of on top of it so you are being affected by the drag of the rip much more. If you stay on top of your board at least you've got a chance to paddle away from the rip. Or else just hold on to your board and wait for help. I would talk not only about the ocean, but also about flat water dangers – quarries, pits, canals and that kind of thing. I'd also tell them not to jump into water unless they could see what's below the surface, because that's how people can get their legs trapped, or get spiked.

I'd do a little talk about the history of Bilbo's breed and tell stories of heroic Newfoundland rescues. For example, when Napoleon made his famous escape from imprisonment on the island of Elba in 1815 a storm blew up and he was washed overboard by a large wave. A fisherman's Newfoundland jumped into the sea and kept him afloat until they reached safety. The Victorians also took the breed to their hearts. A famous artist, Sir Edwin Landseer, well known for his paintings of animals, painted a picture in 1838 called *Saved*, depicting a black and white Newfoundland with a little boy he had rescued from the sea. It became such a popular and well-known painting in the Victorian era that the black and white Newfoundlands are now called Landseers. The Victorians also liked to bathe in the sea, of course, and it was a big era for Britain's beaches. By-laws at the time stated that resorts like Blackpool, Brighton and Bournemouth had to have a Newfoundland on the beach to rescue people.

Often, when we arrived at a school, the children would be hanging on the playground railings chanting: 'Bilbo . . . Bilbo . . . Bilbo!' We usually spoke to a class of about thirty children, but sometimes we'd appear in front of an entire school, which could be anything up to four hundred kids. One time when we had taken morning assembly at a school in Truro the head teacher said to me afterwards, 'I don't think I've ever seen that before, where three hundred and eighty children sat still for thirty-five minutes without fidgeting!' They were completely bewitched by Bilbo.

They wanted to know everything about him: how much he weighed (twelve and a half stone), how tall he was (3 feet) and how long (5 foot 7). In the early days I would get Bilbo to stand on his back legs and put his paws on my chest so they could see his height when upright. I'm just over six foot and Bilbo was about five eleven – they always enjoyed that bit! But I stopped him from doing that because I realized it probably wasn't a good thing to have all that weight on his hindquarters. I was in the vet's one day and saw a model skeleton of a dog. I noticed that there only appears to be one small bone connecting their hind legs, so it's a very delicate part of their anatomy.

Some of the children's questions were a hoot. I remember when we were at a school in Tintagel and we were having a question and answer session. There was a boy sitting at the back of the class and his eyes, riveted upon Bilbo, were getting bigger and bigger. Finally, he could contain himself no longer. He put his hand up and when I asked him if he wanted to ask a question about Bilbo he said, stuttering, 'C-C-Can he fly?'

Another little girl in the same class wanted to know what would happen if she got into trouble in the sea and Bilbo swam out to rescue her as she was allergic to dogs. 'I don't think you'd be worrying about your allergies if you were going to drown,' I said, thinking to myself: That would be the least of your problems!

But then Bilbo had a wonderful effect on even the most timid children. When we visited John Daniels School in Penzance, a school for children with physical or learning difficulties, the youngsters were literally cowering in fear when Bilbo arrived. They had their backs pressed against the wall when we went in, but within half an hour they were fussing Bilbo and crawling all over him. He was so gentle with them that even the kids who were terrified of dogs forgot about it after a while.

He was showered with gifts, naturally. Usually when we arrived there was one of those huge 'Bilbo-sized' rawhide bones, which they'd give him. The school often asked in advance what his favourite treats were and would have a packet waiting for him.

Bilbo did show me up on occasion, though. I never had him neutered and he did go through a phase of trying to hump things. One time we were visiting a school in Newlyn and this little boy and girl asked if they could walk Bilbo round the playground at break-time. I was a bit dubious and said, 'Well, he's very strong, you know.' But they said, 'Oh, please, we're just in the playground.'

'Go on then,' I said. So they took him and of course Bilbo immediately turned round and started humping the boy! I had to rush over and try to cover it up and make it look as if nothing was happening. 'He's just being over friendly,' I told the kid. 'He does that because we wrestle a lot.' It was so embarrassing. I dread to think what he told his parents he'd learnt at school that day! But that was a rare occurrence, I'm pleased to say.

After our talk we would have a session where they got to touch Bilbo for themselves. Sometimes we would have three hundred school kids queuing up to pat him. They could roll him over and fuss him like a bear and he'd be loving it – he just accepted it as his due!

Afterwards they each got a certificate that said: 'This is to certify that (child's name) has met Bilbo.' At the top was Bilbo's picture and the words 'Bilbo Says Swim Between the Flags'. There'd also be an imprint of his enormous paw, which Bilbo had done personally. I had previously bought an ink pad and he had patiently allowed me to take his paw print. He didn't mind, he knew it was for his fans. The kids loved how big that was! Afterwards they did projects with their teachers and created wall displays for their classrooms with Bilbo and the Lifeguard Service as their central theme. They'd draw and paint pictures of Bilbo, some of which were more anatomically correct than others!

Later we would often get a letter from the head teacher, thanking us for visiting and letting us know how helpful it had been for the children, and of course the kids wrote us thank you letters too. More often than not these would be addressed to Bilbo. They would say things like, 'Please tell your dad how much we enjoyed having you both here.' Sometimes my name appeared as an afterthought in brackets: 'Dear Bilbo (and Steve)'! Only occasionally, if I was lucky, would a letter begin 'Dear J'mo'.

Some of the letters we received were a scream. One boy sent me two pages, saying how much he had enjoyed our visit, and finished it by saying: 'Finally, I thank you for wasting your time by coming into our school.' Just priceless!

Bilbo's visits certainly lived on in the children's memories. One of the first schools we went to was Ludgvan Primary School, near Penzance. We went back six months later and the kids were all sitting there in their red shorts and yellow shirts, waving red and yellow flags. They'd remembered everything we'd been talking about – it was great. Another time a letter arrived at Chez Noir from the head teacher of Mount Charles School, near St Austell. 'Although it has been two years since you and Bilbo visited, the children haven't stopped talking about him,' she wrote. The youngsters had organized a cake sale and had raised some money, which they wanted to go 'towards Bilbo's food and upkeep'. Enclosed was a cheque for £17.60. I found that so moving.

11

There's a Bear in My Garden!

Bilbo kept up his ardent pursuit of female canines and led both Mark and me a merry dance on many an occasion. He ran away from Mark when he was looking after him at his house in Hayle twice. We found both incidents amusing in hindsight – although they weren't funny for the people involved!

One balmy afternoon around teatime in late October as the day's sea breeze was falling away, Mark and his girl-friend at the time were bringing the shopping in from the car. Bilbo was so big you'd think you couldn't miss him, but he was nonetheless capable of sneaking around – 'like a sniper' as Mark put it. Anyway, they'd unpacked the groceries and suddenly thought: Where the hell's Bilbo?

'He'd just disappeared,' Mark relayed to me later. 'It must have been when we left the door pulled to.' He ran out into the street and heard an ear-piercing scream, which he knew instantly was somehow connected to Bilbo. It transpired that the blighter had gone down to the end of the street and round the back where a grass field backed onto some houses. He jumped a woman's fence and by the time Mark got there he was busy humping her golden Labrador in the yard. The poor woman, meanwhile, thought a bear had jumped over her fence and was eating her dog, and had locked herself in the garden shed.

'I jumped over straight away and grabbed him and was thinking, How do we get out of here?' Mark said, laughing. 'The woman peered round the corner of her shed door and said, "Oh my God, I thought it was a bear!" But she still carried on screaming for ages, even though she realized he was a dog. It took her ages to calm down.'

She may have been hysterical, but the unfortunate woman was not the first to mistake Bilbo for a wild animal. I realized early on that I had to make sure I knew where Bilbo was all the time because a lot of people really did think he was a bear, and you don't want to meet a bear coming towards you on the cliff path at dusk!

We came to learn that when you were out for a walk with Bilbo his body language would change when he smelled female dogs, which he had a particular nose for. He'd adopt a lacklustre walk, as if to say, 'Well, I didn't really want to come out,' and would start acting all jittery, as if he knew what he was about to do was wrong. And then off he'd dash.

One time Mark was walking him at Mexico Towans beach, near his home, because it was a good place to let him off the lead as you could see a long way into the distance and it would be hard to lose him. Or so he thought. But on this particular occasion Bilbo smelled the fairer sex and legged it. Mark set off in hot pursuit but despite being a young, fit lifeguard he was no match for Bilbo – especially an amorous Bilbo!

He finally caught up with him in an adjacent street where, once again, he had followed the sound of human female screaming. 'Bilbo had run down the street and jumped a stable door into this woman's house and was harassing her German shepherd in the kitchen when I caught up with him,' he laughed. Mark was left to make profuse apologies and shamefacedly had to drag Bilbo out in disgrace.

Despite his size and weight, Bilbo had no trouble jumping. He was amazingly nimble when he wanted to be and used to jump up onto the veranda at our lifeguard hut, which was over a metre high – a huge jump for any dog. He cleared a five-bar gate when he was ten, and that was a similar height. He had his rope leash on at the time so he was lucky he didn't throttle himself. I had to watch him all the time – that's why he could be such hard work, because you did have to keep a constant eye on him.

I was lucky that I had a willing dog-sitter in Mark. Not that I normally had cause to go away. I am not one for holidays. Living down here is so wonderful, where would I possibly want to go? I did visit Barbados once, in the eighties. A group of us went on a surfing trip to Bathsheba, on the island's east coast, and ended up staying for four months. It was great – I loved it. But other than that I was content with my 'Golden Triangle' – beach, pub and home – down here at Land's End.

But with the summer over and the weather turning colder, my thoughts turned to Shetland. I missed home and Mum and that year, like most others, I visited her in October around my birthday. I always looked forward to seeing her and to going home, but I never looked forward to the journey. It could be done in a day if you flew, but that involved having five stops: Newquay–Gatwick–Heathrow–Edinburgh–Aberdeen–Shetland. Plus it cost the proverbial arm and a leg.

It took two days by train to Aberdeen, and then I'd have to take either the plane or a fourteen-hour ferry to Shetland. The other option, car and ferry, also took at least two days each way. When they were little the kids used to love the adventure of going to Shetland because it would be a different journey every time and was inevitably fraught with hiccups. Suffice to say, there was no way I was going to inflict such a journey on Bilbo. It just wouldn't have been fair.

How well I remember the first time I had to entrust Bilbo to Mark. Having told Bilbo faithfully that I would never leave him, here I was about to do just that. Not only that, but we had just spent our first five months together in a working capacity having been with each other twenty-four hours every day!

But making my annual trip north to visit Mum for two weeks was important to me and there was just *no* way Bilbo could accompany me. Mark of course was straining at the leash to have Bilbo to stay, whereas I was at the other end of the spectrum – worried and wondering how he would cope with not seeing me for over a fortnight. Would Mark look after him? Did Mark even know what 'looking after' him meant?

'Listen, Corn Fed,' I said (one of Mark's many nicknames, given on account of him looking so well nourished and, as he would say, 'buff'). 'Bilbo can be *very* naughty if you don't keep him under control and that means knowing *where* he is and what he is up to at *all* times. If things should go quiet suddenly, investigate what is going on *immediately*!'

'Don't worry, Captain,' Mark replied, a cheeky grin already spreading across his face. 'He will be just fine here with me.'

'Hmm, that's precisely what I am worried about,' I replied. 'The pair of you together and me over one thousand miles away – what could possibly go wrong?!'

And so it was that I loaded Bilbo and his luggage into the 4x4 and reluctantly drove away from Chez Noir, the setting sun glowing blood red on the distant horizon behind us. Bilbo never missed a trick and had already taken note of the day's goings-on. He watched as I packed up his bedding, towels and so on, following me to the car each time. 'It's OK, Billy. Everything is fine,' I assured him. 'You are such a good boy – *MY BOY*.' But he had already twigged something was happening and became extremely clingy for the rest of the afternoon.

Arriving at Mark's, Bilbo jumped out, his tail wagging, glad to see Mark. Phew, I thought. At least he is pleased to see him. As I unloaded the car, I noticed Bilbo becoming a bit anxious, trying to climb back in.

'Here, I'll take him for an evening stroll,' said Mark to take Bilbo's mind off things. Emptying the car, I said goodbye to Bilbo, trying hard to be as nonchalant as I could. But the truth was I was tearing up inside at the prospect of leaving him. Bilbo was occupied with getting ready to go out with Mark and I took the opportunity to slip away. Looking in the rear-view mirror I could see them both standing there, Bilbo with his big tail slowly wagging from side to side, and my heart felt very heavy indeed.

I was due to leave for Shetland early the next morning so I switched my attention to the journey and the two weeks ahead. Mark had my mobile number as well as my mother's landline. I knew he would call me if needs be, so I felt safe in the knowledge that Bilbo was OK and in good hands.

That night, back in Chez Noir, I noticed just how empty and quiet it was without my sidekick. Not a good feeling, I decided.

But the fortnight passed relatively quickly and without any news from Mark. I had already instructed him only to phone me in emergencies because, in my book, no news is good news.

When, at long last, I arrived at Mark's to pick Bilbo up, he was a picture. Mark had groomed him and he smelled of coconut shampoo! I was thrilled to see him looking so happy. His face was all scrunched up, and he was snuffling and sneezing with excitement, as was his way. I had laid out the rear of the 4x4 with clean towels and he was up and in there as soon as I opened the door. Driving back down our lane to Chez Noir, he had his head stuck out of the window, ears flapping in the gentle sea air. He was glad to be home and the feeling was mutual.

Luckily Mark loved having Bilbo to stay – although his allure soon waned with his girlfriend . . . Mark is a bit of a prankster; he used to enjoy winding her up by calling Bilbo upstairs at seven in the morning and getting him to jump on the bed. She'd be half asleep and Mark would give Bilbo the hand signal to jump and this massive dog would leap on the bed and crush the poor girl, to the point where she couldn't move. Bilbo would just be standing on the bed, pinning her down with the quilt. Mark, needless to say, found it hilarious.

One morning, however, Bilbo refused to get on the bed. 'It was really weird,' he told me. 'I tried for ten minutes to get him to wind her up but he was all flustered and walking round the room.' The reason the poor lad was loath to get on the duvet was soon horribly apparent. He turned round at the end of the bed and brushed his bottom against the radiator, leaving an unpleasant brown mark on the wall. 'She must have fed him something bad because he'd pooed himself and it was all caught on his fur,' said Mark. 'But what was really good was the fact that he wouldn't jump on the bed. And paradoxically she began to like him after that because she imagined the mess she would have had to clear up if he had jumped all over her bed linen!'

You get the picture: in Mark's eyes at least, Bilbo could do no wrong.

12

Lifesaver

Most of our school visits took place during the months leading up to the summer holidays. However, when I was in Shetland, Mark had a request to take Bilbo to do a talk on beach safety. He thought he would only be there for an hour but ended up getting roped in to stay the whole day because it was the feast day of St Francis, the patron saint of animals – hence why Bilbo had been invited.

'They invited us up onto the stage in assembly and it was proper embarrassing, J'mo,' he complained to me afterwards. 'I felt like a pillock because I had to spend all day in a pair of tight shorts and a lifeguard top. When we went into dinner I had to sit on one of those little mini chairs! And I had to have Bilbo with me the whole time because there was nowhere to put him, so he was there drooling all over the kids' dinners.'

On a more serious note, I was always at pains to point out to the children that just because someone was wearing a top saying 'lifeguard', it didn't mean they were one. The surf shacks and gift shops sold T-shirts with 'Lifeguard' emblazoned across, and I was alert to the fact that a paedophile could masquerade as one of us and potentially take a child from the beach. So I always said to the youngsters that a lifeguard would never attempt to take them away from the beach, and if anyone ever tried to get them to go with them to the shops or the car park, they were to say in a loud voice, 'No! You're not a proper lifeguard – leave me alone!' I told them that if they shouted loud enough, they would be left alone.

'The only place a proper lifeguard will ever take you is to the lifeguard hut, where Bilbo might be and you can stroke him and give him a fuss and we can use the big binoculars to look for your mum and dad,' I'd tell them.

We could have up to three hundred lost children in a season on Sennen; we were always reuniting youngsters with their parents. It sounds a lot, but it's understandable when you think there could be seven thousand people on the beach some days. On holiday people behave differently. The usual safety concerns go out the window because some parents are busy having fun, or they fall asleep in the sun. I'd see kids wandering around on their own and ask them, 'Where are your mum and dad?' And they'd inevitably say, 'I'm lost.' Sometimes they could be at the hut for half an hour before anyone came looking for them.

It's amazing how far a toddler can walk in twenty minutes. I remember a two-year-old who walked right across Sennen beach. It was low tide so he went in front of the rocks and was on Gwynver beach when he was found. He'd walked the best part of half a mile. There were loads of people on the beach that day, but no one had taken any notice of him.

The instinctive protective qualities of the Newfoundland breed meant that Bilbo's awareness was constant and he was always on the lookout. Because we lived just above the beach, one of our favourite walks was along the beautiful coastal path towards Cape Cornwall. Lots of dogs would accompany walkers along the five-mile stretch and Bilbo was in heaven – he didn't know where to start sniffing first!

It was on one of these walks at the end of the summer season when Bilbo's instinct took over. Although the sun was shining, there was a fresh onshore breeze and a heavy groundswell running. The sun's rays still held some warmth and a few people were sitting in the lee of rocks here and there. I had noticed two small children, both fully clothed, down at the water's edge with no obvious parent or guardian about. I was concerned as the swell had particularly large 'set' waves within it and these children were only around primary school age.

'That's not a good situation for those children to be in,' I said to Bilbo. They were running down the beach with the wave as it receded and, as more waves broke, they would race them back up again. All very well, you may think, but if those children were to be caught by a big set wave, the water is going to rush in faster than they can run away from it. People can easily be knocked over by rushing water and potentially be dragged into the sea.

As I stood there working out the best thing to do, Bilbo took off back along the cliff path to the beach. He was down there within seconds and stood between the children and the water, preventing them from getting near the waves. This gave me enough time to get down there myself and find the parents. I said to them: 'You see that dog over there, do you see what he's doing?' They looked at me, bemused, and said, 'What? No. Why?' They didn't understand the danger, but Bilbo had!

I said: 'You don't even know what your children are doing, do you?' Having witnessed some of the things that can happen to unsupervised children, I would get upset when adults didn't know where their children were, or what they were doing on the beach. One of my friends recounted a story of when she was on Porthcurno beach and a young child was going towards the sea unaccompanied. The lifeguard kept saying to the mother, 'Look, it is too rough for him to be in there,' but she just ignored him. 'Leave me alone, will you, I'm trying to sleep!' she yelled finally. They had to get the police down there in the end.

I've seen fully clothed children taken off the beach at high tide by a wave. Surf beaches are rarely flat and at high tide you'll get these undulations in the sand, so there will be peaks and troughs. I've seen when a wave has gone up and come back down behind them and the force of the foam has swept them into the sea. Janus and I had to rescue two little children and an adult on one occasion. The children got washed into the sea and because there was swell there was a rip right next to the beach and they were five metres off the shore within seconds.

We saw it all happen. We were just getting changed, as we had not even officially started work. We charged across the beach in our Speedos just to get to them in time. The father had also seen what had happened and had jumped in after them. Now he was caught up in the rip and was in as much trouble as they were. The little boy, who was only about seven, was really brave. He held his sister's head up, treading water as best he could. But hang on to her he did!

She was only about five years old. I went for the children and towed them ashore while Janus rescued the father.

That particular occasion was before Bilbo's time, but later on, when he was four years old, Bilbo's instinctive desire to help those in trouble kicked in. We were doing some pre-season water training. It was a lovely sunny Sennen day and there were a few people about as well as the local surf school giving a lesson. During a break in our training, I was chatting to some friends who had just returned to Sennen for the coming season. 'Where's Bilbo?' one of them asked.

Looking around, I saw him further down the beach, barking away, and some of the surf school staff running over to where he was. A young girl had been bowled over by oncoming set waves. She was caught up in the washing machine effect and couldn't regain her footing. I ran towards them but Bilbo's barking had alerted surfers who were closer by. They ran into the sea and managed to haul the girl out of the surf. Bilbo kept barking until the little girl was sitting on the sand, gasping and spluttering. She was none the worse for her near-drowning experience but it was a lucky escape and Bilbo had come to the rescue.

I didn't give it too much thought at the time but, years later, Bilbo and I were in the Swordfish Inn in Newlyn, when this girl shouted out and came over to give Bilbo a hug. 'He saved me! He saved me!' she said. I smiled quietly and proudly to myself.

Many holidaymakers came back year after year and got to know us well. They would sit and chat to the lifeguards and we became like family to some of them. Each year over 250,000 people visit Sennen and Bilbo was a hit with the tourists right from the start. Some of them would come every year just to see him. Because of the official dog ban on Sennen beach, Bilbo and I would only go onto the beach once or twice a day to advertise when he would be doing his next rescue demonstration. It was on these occasions when he would meet new children who would then come to visit him at the lifeguard hut daily, giving us a great opportunity for some beach awareness education. One of these was a young girl from Portsmouth called Laura, who has returned to Cornwall every year since 2005 when she first met Bilbo. She was seven or eight when she first met him and she's about seventeen now. And there was a little girl called Yasmin who came from Turkey one year and befriended Bilbo. She bought him ice creams and still keeps in touch.

They would send Bilbo Christmas and birthday cards. From 2006 onwards he started to get loads of mail and quite often the envelope would just say: 'Bilbo, Sennen, Cornwall'. I kept all the letters and cards, along with the children's drawings and friendly notes, complete with their enchanting spelling mistakes. 'I loved it when Bilbo did his trik,' wrote one little boy after we'd been to his school. That was because when we were leaving the school I'd say to Bilbo, 'Atten-shun!' and if he was lying down he'd sit up straight. The kids loved that.

'There are not many dogs that you cheer and play with like Bilbo,' wrote one child. And one of my favourites, which came from a young girl: 'If you're looking for a new friend, find Bilbo because he's the best one for it.'

She was right about that. He'd certainly become my best friend, as I told the television crews that began arriving with increasing frequency to film Bilbo in action. His fame had spread far and wide. I was contacted by St John Radio from Newfoundland in Canada, who were naturally interested in knowing more about Bilbo the lifeguard dog, and a documentary team travelled from Germany to make a television programme about us. They filmed us at home in Chez Noir and shot footage of Bilbo with sunglasses on, surrounded by adoring children on the beach. It was just unbelievable the amount of attention he got.

I was on the beach one day with Bilbo when this chap stopped me and said, 'I didn't know you could speak Thai, J'mo.' I was bemused for a second, and he continued: 'I've just come back from Thailand and was in this bar there when you and the King here flashed up on the screen. You were being interviewed about something, how cool was that? I had quite a few free drinks that night on the back of that one! So thanks, J'mo, mate.'

For my part, I had no idea our interviews were being broadcast so far away. My dog had become a fully fledged celebrity and was loving every minute of it. And, if I'm honest, so was I. And this was just the beginning . . .

13

War Wounds

Bilbo and I settled in for our first winter together and life at Chez Noir was pretty hard-core during the coldest months. Our mornings soon followed a familiar pattern: we made our way into the front room and huddled together under a blanket, me with a cup of tea in my hands, as we gathered our thoughts before the morning's walk.

And although Bilbo was already starting to become a celebrity, there was no time for him to get big-headed. After all, he was a working dog and there was hard work to be done every day. As well as going round the unmanned beaches to check on the lifesaving equipment, it was our job, Bilbo's and mine, to make sure they were also clear of rubbish, which we did as we watched the fishing boats heading out to sea. A lot of what we collected was jetsam from fishing boats and although I could not condone the dumping of rubbish at sea, having been there I understand how it can happen. There was also lots and lots of plastic. Two years before I got Bilbo, a ship – the RMS *Mulheim* – ran aground near Land's End in March 2003, spilling just over two thousand tonnes of shredded plastic from scrapped

Mike and me. Gwynver, 1978.

Here I am in the 1980s.

Some of the 'Legendary Penwith Lifeguards' in the 1970s.

We're not worried. Bilbo was always great with sheep.

Bilbo with his pals, the Chez Noir chicks.

Bilbo was most at home in the great outdoors.

Majestic Bilbo. He loved the smell of daffodils.

Beach training,
June 2006.

On duty at Sennen
Cove.

Me (centre) with
Billy and the boys
on Sennen.

Ever watchful. Our base
at Sennen.

Chauffeur-driven. Riding
pillion with me on the quad.

Billy standing tall.

Staying focused with his binoculars at the ready.

Bilbo aged twelve. Such a handsome boy.

Bilbo looking down on his beloved Gwynver.

Back on board after a cooling swim.

Overleaf
My best friend and constant companion.

cars into the sea near Sennen. Although there was a clean-up of sorts, most of the cargo was lost into the sea and still appears on Sennen beach to this day.

An occasional potential danger was that of incendiary devices being washed up, because the Ministry of Defence had dumped a whole lot of them out in the Western Approaches after the Second World War. And there were other hazards. For all the locals' talk of there being quicksand on Gwynver, it wasn't bottomless quicksand – it's purely that the sand is so waterlogged from the amount of current and waves that hit that beach, you can walk along and suddenly sink up to your thighs. You're not going to totally disappear, but the sand is so full of water it can feel quite scary.

And in the rip area on beaches is where you also find the weaver fish. They are one of the main hazards on these beaches. You don't hear a lot about them, but every year hundreds of people get stung. They have poisonous spines on their back and are about ten to fifteen centimetres long, although there are larger ones up to about forty centimetres long found in the sea. Horrible as they may be, they can be a great advantage to a lifeguard if he's got any kind of nous about him. Obviously we don't want people going in where the rips are, but bathers often head for the rip because it *looks* calm to the untrained eye. However, the sand around the rips is usually waterlogged and that's where most of these fish lie, waiting for the tide to come back in. They hear the vibration of people's feet coming along so they put their spines up to protect themselves, and of course people step on them. We would soon know when that happened, as they would be on the beach, hobbling around, or someone would be carrying them up to the life-guard hut – usually in tears of pain.

So, if we informed beachgoers of the weaver fish, they would stay away from wet, soft sand at the water's edge. The fishes' spines are tipped with a poison which the spine 'injects' into the casualty's foot when stepped on. I've seen one sticking out of somebody's foot and there was even an instance where a bather sat on one! The poison is a protein and, like an egg white, sets when heated up. So, if you warm the affected part, it prevents the poison from spreading up the leg. As the spring and early summer arrived and people were out barefoot on the beaches again, we were constantly boiling kettles because there would be a continual stream of them coming to the hut. Some days would be worse than others. The treatment was pretty painful too. Weaver casualties would be asked to sit with their feet in a bowl of hot water, as hot as they could bear, for anything up to twenty minutes – the water constantly being topped up.

Luckily Bilbo never stepped on one, but then he was on the quad bike most of the time. In thirty-four years on the beach I thought I'd got away with it, until 2009 when I stood on one and it really was quite painful.

Over the years I have sustained a few injuries and have had to deal with pain. However, I feel lucky as I seem to have quite a high threshold for it. I also learnt that following a major trauma to a part of the body, there is a (relatively) pain-free window of about a minute in which to act and do what has to be done. And Rule One is: keep a clear head. Once, when shooting a long line, a fishing hook became embedded in the fleshy part of my hand as the line was paying out over the side of the boat, almost taking me with it. I quickly cut the strop, which attached the hook to the line, but was left with a fairly large hook still in my hand. The skipper said: 'You'll want to get that out right away, boy, otherwise in a couple of minutes you won't be able to touch it.' Trusting his judgement, and gritting my teeth, I wrestled it out with relative ease, all things considered. Then it was a case of patching up the wound – the pain came later.

It was the same in 2005 when I broke my ankle on a beach on Tiree, a remote island in the Inner Hebrides. I was providing lifeguard and first aid cover at a big windsurfing event, the 'Tiree Wave Classic'. Tiree is one of the most exposed islands and is billed as the windiest and sunniest of the Hebridean chain. Anyway, one day during the contest there was no wind and the event was put on hold. It was a lovely sunny day and the competitors were out on the beach, enjoying the autumn sun. Someone produced these little monkey bikes and loads of guys were racing up and down the mile-long, flat beach. One fellow kept urging me to ride one of them: 'Go on, J'mo, have a go on the monkey bike!'

Those vehicles only have a 49cc single four-stroke engine, with the seat less than sixty centimetres off the ground. I had a road bike of my own at the time and was saying: 'Look, what's the point of riding that thing flat out up and down the beach? I already ride a motorbike; I've no wish to go on it!'

Later on in the afternoon he was still going on and on, and in the end I said, 'For God's sake, give us the bike then.' I didn't take much notice of it at the time, but on one side it seemed as if half of the footrest had been broken off.

Anyway, reluctantly I got on this thing and took off over some rough ground to get down to the hard sand. I was only doing about ten to fifteen miles per hour when suddenly the front wheel dug in, my foot slipped off the footrest, hit the floor and I went straight over the handlebars. I landed with a thud and just lay there for a second while I checked out my limbs. And when I saw my right foot I was dismayed. It was limply hanging to one side at a horrible angle. I couldn't feel much, but still I knew that it was not good. I was concerned about circulation and I knew I had to straighten the foot – and quickly. Where I was there was no hospital, no resident doctor – nothing.

I knew of this window of about thirty seconds to a minute where I wouldn't really feel the pain and I just sat there and thought: Right, well I've got to do it, because if I don't the blood flow could be cut off to my foot. And that was not good, as gangrene could set in and I would risk losing my foot altogether. And I knew enough about that to know it could happen really quickly.

So I decided to do it. Remembering what the skipper had said to me all those years ago, I gathered myself and grasped hold of my foot and firmly hoicked it back into position. The sensation was so bad I nearly passed out, but it was the right thing to do. They had to fly in a private jet to the little airfield on Tiree and airlift me to Glasgow Southern General in the middle of the night. I was in there for three days and have a metal plate in my leg to this day.

When I lost my left index finger I didn't feel any pain at all to begin with. My surfing leash had got wrapped round it and a big wave just snapped it off. It was a dismal day and there was no one on the beach so Janus and I had decided to go for a surf because the waves were quite big. But as we were getting changed we saw this chap stood at the water's edge with a long board.

I thought there was no way he would get off the beach – because the surf was so big. But of course, Sod's Law, you get lulls where it goes quiet for a little while and he jumped in during one of those lulls. And the next thing we saw he was paddling out towards where the rip was. I knew if he got involved with that there was only one place he was going to end up, and that was in the impact zone. And you don't want to be in the impact zone with a long board. You can be taken out onto the sandbank where the waves are just full of sand. They are heavy as anything and will mash you up and could snap your board and give you a beating.

So we had to get to him fast and persuade him to go back in to the beach. We managed to get him to turn round, and he was paddling back to the beach when I looked and saw that there was another monster set of waves coming in. I held my leash close to my board, so as not to let it shoot forward and hit him because he was only just ahead of me. But I was in the impact zone myself now and got washing-machined in the waves. Thankfully, the guy was pushed into the beach because the wave had already broken, whereas I got pushed down onto the seabed.

What the waves do, if they are big, is hold you down. The first wave breaks on top of you and pushes you down to the bottom, and the momentum of the water pushing in won't allow you up. The next wave comes and pushes you down again, and so on. I could feel my board up the top somewhere doing what we call tomb-stoning – poking up vertically through the water – and I could feel the leash stretching, getting thinner and thinner. I thought: It's going to snap any minute now . . . And at that moment it just went *ping!* I thought I heard it, but I couldn't have really, not over the sound of the waves.

At that stage, I was just thinking that I'd lost my board and it was going to be a massive swim back to the beach. So when I surfaced and my board was there, I thought: Fantastic! But when I reached out my hand to get it I felt only horror as I looked at my finger. Or should I say where my finger *should* have been. Grabbing the base of the finger with my thumb and third finger, I paddled in to the beach. I didn't feel the pain until I got to the lifeguard hut and was trying to get in the door – which, as bad luck would have it, was padlocked. The painkillers were inside and it took me ages to unlock the door and get to them. I stood there, cursing the padlock and squeezing the stump as hard as I could to stop the blood flowing.

Yet, even though life tried me at times, I never doubted the wisdom of leaving the corporate world behind for a job in the great outdoors.

14

The Pied Piper

Along with the many cards and letters from Bilbo's growing fan club, invitations to VIP gatherings started to land on the mat at Chez Noir. Not for me, I hasten to add, but for 'His Nibs'.

The first big event he was asked to be guest of honour at was the Hayne Dog Jamboree in September 2006. It was held at Moreton Hampstead, a village on Dartmoor, in the grounds of a big country house called Hayne Old Manor, which was owned by the Constantine family. The organizers wrote to me to say they had heard about Bilbo, and asked if he would appear at their show. It was in aid of local charities, including the Devon Air Ambulance; the Sir Francis Chichester Trust for Youth, a charity that sends children on outward-bound courses; and Rapid UK, a search and rescue volunteer group. In return they would be happy to make a donation to our lifeguard service.

Naturally, I was more than happy to agree and was ridiculously proud to see that Bilbo had 'Special Celebrity Appearance' billing on the show programme. Mark, Bilbo and I went to check the venue out a few days before and when we saw that it had a lake I had the bright idea of saying, 'We can do a demonstration in the lake and show how Bilbo can rescue people.' I hadn't noticed at this point that there were some black swans residing on said lake, but of course Bilbo clocked them immediately and to his mind it was a case of: 'Game on!' Within seconds he'd dived into the lake and was swimming after the poor swans. There were quite a lot of them – at least twenty – and they were hissing at him, and trying to attack him. Bilbo turned and looked at me, thinking: Mmm, maybe I won't go near them after all . . . and turned back in our direction.

The jamboree was on a warm, sunny early autumn Saturday in September. The idea was that we would do two water displays for the one-thousand-strong crowd. Well, Bilbo was full of beans on the day, leaping up and down, yelping and making a right old racket. I quickly walked him away from the crowd and tried to have a word with him in an attempt to calm him. It was like trying to get a teenager to see reason! 'Billy, you dare show us up here and it will be the last time!' I chided him. 'There will be *no more* ice cream!' Looking at him I knew he was just thinking: Get on with it. We then turned back towards the lake where Mark had already slipped out into the reed beds about thirty metres from the bank. Mark's girlfriend was talking on the megaphone, explaining the proposed sequence of events to the expectant crowd.

As they all watched, rapt, Mark swam out into the middle of the lake and began waving his arm from side to side. Bilbo immediately spotted the arm movement and became instantly fully charged. Strength oozing from him, he bounded into the lake, swimming out with the Peterson tube to Mark, and towed him successfully ashore to great applause.

Mark said he found it a bit daunting, though, because while he was waiting in the reed beds ready to swim out and be rescued, the menacing-looking black swans were staring at him with their beady eyes, as if to say: 'Who the hell are you?'

Later, we were also scheduled to do several laps of the showground with Bilbo on the quad, looking, as Mark put it, 'like a couple of plonkers'. Us, that is, not Bilbo; he always looked very regal on the quad, with his head held high and his fur flying in the breeze. We drove around the arena, stopping every now and then for Bilbo to meet his people. Little wonder I came to call him the King! He enjoyed the crowds; I could tell because he would always get excited when we were going to do something like that. He would be looking around him, because he knew people would pat him and give him treats. He thought he was a celebrity, and of course he was.

When we were getting him ready to go and meet his adoring public, he would often adopt what Mark called his 'proud pose'. And he always looked straight at the camera. If someone was shouting: 'Over here!' he would spot the camera and look towards it. He was brilliant like that. When he was young, I had trained him to sit and pose for the cameras because, right from the start, everyone we met wanted a picture of him.

There was a dog-grooming trailer at the jamboree and the woman offered to shampoo him for free after his swim. She put the word out that she was going to be washing Bilbo the famous lifeguard dog so lots of people would come and watch. It was quite funny to see how small Bilbo became when wet, and he looked at me as if to say: 'Really? I have to endure this again? I didn't smell anyway.' He didn't like being bathed but he tolerated it. Fortunately he didn't try and run out of the booth or anything.

Between demonstrations Mark and myself set up this stall affair, not just to advertise our lifeguard service but also to draw in children to get them engaged with Bilbo and learn a bit about the beach at the same time. We dressed up a gazebo with beach flags and had Bilbo sitting majestically on the quad bike. Suddenly, out of the throng of people surrounding Bilbo, this chap came over and presented me with a beautifully crafted, hand-tooled leather leash. It had brass catches and strategically placed brass rings with two hand loops for better control. 'I used to be a dog handler and just watching your demonstration I was very impressed,' he announced. 'I would like to present you and Bilbo with this. I've just made it,' he added, handing the leash over to me. I was both surprised and very grateful. 'Thank you so much,' I said, shaking his hand. 'I'll put it on him straight away.' We then both stood back and admired him as he sat there looking even more regal.

It was funny at these dog shows because people seemed to think I was the Cornish equivalent of the Dog Whisperer, Cesar Millan. They'd ask: 'What training methods did you bring him up on?' and Mark and I would just look at each other and laugh because we were pretty much winging it.

The jamboree was such a big success that we were invited back the following year. The second time there was even more of a crowd because people had come especially to see Bilbo. But on that occasion it went a bit wrong when we were about to do the lake rescue because yours truly fell over. I had bare feet and the grass was wet and Bilbo was itching to get in the water. He pulled me over and I ended up going head over heels on the ground as the onlookers howled with laughter. To make matters worse, Bilbo was still tied to the quad as well and the quad and I were skiing down the grass bank towards the lake at an alarming speed. Eventually I managed to scramble to my feet in the mud and at the last second I hurriedly untied Bilbo before he dragged the quad and me into the water.

Of course he immediately ran into the lake and – to this day I can't remember exactly how it happened – everyone suddenly started letting their dogs off as well. People were saying, 'I want my dog to swim with Bilbo!' and all these dogs just piled into the lake en masse. And I'm talking everybody – the whole dog show. For his part, Bilbo was just thinking: I'm going after the swans. And he swam right past Mark, not bothering to save him. 'Cheers, Bilbo,' he muttered as he went by.

From the shore I had a brilliant view of Bilbo swimming at the front, like a canine Pied Piper, with dogs of all shapes and sizes doggy-paddling after him. There were tiny dogs, big dogs, spaniels – the lot. It was chaos! The lady who owned the house was crying, 'No, no, no!' but people carried on letting their dogs off and they were all happily swimming away into the sunset. It was an amazing scene.

After the fiasco of Bilbo's lake 'rescue' the parade of the local hunt was scheduled, with all the toffs in their red coats on horseback with the hounds. But because everyone was at the lake with their dogs, no one was in the field, where they were supposed to run around with their pets and pretend to be 'hunted'. Bilbo's antics had messed up the timings for the whole jamboree. The show was running forty-five minutes behind for the rest of the day. Funnily enough we weren't invited back. The family sold the house after that. I don't know if the two events were connected in any way!

Even so, Bilbo's fame was spreading far and wide. His next starring role was in a TV documentary, *Extraordinary Animals: SOS Dog Squad*, featuring alongside a fire rescue dog and one that worked in mountain rescue. And Bilbo's work promoting beach safety in schools led to him being awarded a trophy by the Hayle Rotarians in 2006 when they voted him Dog of the Year. I don't think they *usually* had a dog of the year; I think it was invented just for him. It was a case of them acknowledging the public service he was providing, and I was really pleased that we were being appreciated.

We became involved in more and more events. It meant I was away from the beach quite a bit but it was great publicity for the lifeguarding service and I was happy to roll with it. A friend of ours wanted to raise money for Macmillan Cancer Support after his wife tragically died of the disease and we said we'd bring Bilbo down to help boost awareness. The Newlyn to Penzance race is an open-water sea swim. The race is approximately 1,300 metres and you usually have a good mix of competitors taking part – triathletes, sea swimmers and lifeguards. Mark and I thought that if Bilbo participated it might attract a wider range of people and make it more fun. We weren't intending for him to swim the entire distance, because it might have been just too far. The plan was to take him into the water at the start of the swim and once everyone had swum past we'd take him back to the beach. He might swim as far as the promenade so the spectators could see him, but if he was in the water for only ten seconds, so be it.

Bilbo was – in Mark's words – 'well up for it'. It was a lovely end-of-summer evening. The sun was still shining brightly and the wind had dropped away to a mere breeze. As we approached the muster point there were hundreds of people milling around. Bilbo was prickling with excitement and it was a challenge just to keep hold of him. As for sitting still for the pre-swim group photo, well Bilbo just did not get that bit, although eventually the newspapers got their picture.

There are usually a couple of hundred taking part. There are county swimmers racing one another, there's prize money involved and some people are in it to win, whilst others just do it for a laugh. Everyone lines up at the start and when all the swimmers are in position, a horn is sounded and everyone sets off at once. It's a real bun fight. People are punching one another out of the way to get through because it's so competitive. The start is actually quite challenging, with hundreds of swimmers vying for clear, flat water from a 'standing' start.

We planned to wait with Bilbo on the beach, let everyone go by and then loop in behind them so the crowd could see Bilbo swim. But when all the swimmers set off without him Bilbo went absolutely nuts. He was making loads of noise and practically pulled us into the sea. The sea around our coast at that time of year is almost at its warmest and it was quite a relief for all of us to get in there!

Once we were in the water I swam in front and Mark swam with Bilbo behind me, which is what we normally did in training. After Bilbo had settled he just paddled along, eating every piece of seaweed along the way. I noticed that he was breathing in through his nose and out through his mouth, which was different from how he usually breathed in the water. But then when he swam out to 'rescue' Mark it wasn't very far. Swimming now across the bay from Newlyn, Bilbo was like a little motor, making *phut, phut* noises as he went.

I kept stopping and asking Mark how it was going, and he kept saying, 'Yes, keep going, it's good; it's all good.'

As lifeguards, we had naturally thought about how we would get him out safely at various stages of the swim, just as we would when assessing if a person is in difficulty. We had an action plan for Bilbo should he get tired, or should anything go wrong. We knew there were various ledges along the promenade where we could get him out if we needed to. And we would both be in the water with him. We got past the beach and we'd gone quite far out because I thought if anything did go wrong and Bilbo got into dif-ficulties, we could put the Peterson tube on him and Mark and I could bring him in without worrying the spectators that the famous lifesaving dog might be in trouble. It was just my contingency plan.

But Bilbo just kept going, swimming parallel to the Western Promenade and past the Queen's Hotel. On and on he went, and he ended up doing the whole swim as if it was expected of him all along. He was cheered by the crowds the whole way. They followed him along the prom-enade, shouting, 'Come on Bilbo!' He came in at 31 minutes

2 seconds, which is within the time specified in the life-guard fitness test. And, remember, he had started well behind everyone else.

He was the first dog ever to do that swim and he was presented with a medal just like everyone else who finished. He seemed really proud, because he loved being part of things. Mark was convinced that the swim had had a profound effect on Bilbo. He reckoned something changed in him after that because for about a week afterwards whenever he and I were sitting down, Bilbo had to touch us. He seemed to need physical contact. This was, as Mark put it, 'really weird', because usually when we were at the life-guard hut Bilbo would just go and dig a hole in the sand and lie in it. But Mark was on lookout the day after the swim. He'd set up the comfy cushion and was lying down on his chest when Bilbo came and sat next to him and rested his back paw on Mark's foot.

'I was like, "Get off! What are you doing, you weirdo?"' Mark laughed. 'But then he'd slowly put his paw back on me when I wasn't looking. I think he had bonded that bit closer to us through the experience of the swim. I don't think it had scared him – I think he just knew that he was one of the boys now. And he was really well behaved afterwards, although only for about a week!'

The swim became an annual event for the three of us and Bilbo did it four times in all. No other dog has done it to date. It diversified the event because although the serious competitors still took part, people who weren't that great at swimming were inspired by Bilbo to participate in the race. And because Bilbo beat some of the swimmers – we would overtake quite a few – people started to say: 'I just want to beat the dog.' And when we'd overtake them you could see them thinking: Oh my God, am I doing that badly?

The first couple of years we waited behind the swimmers while they lined up by the wall, because there was a lot of jostling and Bilbo would be going bonkers. They'd all set off in a great froth and then we'd go in and try and catch up with them. But after the second swim it became obvious that Bilbo was getting distressed at the start because he didn't understand what was going on. He was paddling all over the place. I was trying to swim in front of him and I'd look round and think: Where the hell is Bilbo? Perhaps he thought the other swimmers needed saving.

The first two swims went smoothly, but by the third year people would be calling him and chanting his name. And when they started doing that Bilbo thought they were calling him in, so he swam in to the shore and got out a few times. I didn't have any of this hassle because I was the lead swimmer, swimming ahead and trying to give Bilbo something to focus on, because I knew he always caught me up. Mark, meanwhile, had to make several detours to the beach to fetch him back. It was definitely the people shouting that caused him to veer off course. But then knowing how much he loved fame, it was probably also a case of Bilbo thinking he'd just go and sign a few autographs! It wasn't the allure of the Indian restaurant on the way, which overcame one of the swimmers. He was swimming past and could smell the curry wafting across the bay, so he got out of the sea, went in there and ordered a takeaway!

Even the strongest swimmer can get into difficulty in a harbour, and one day in 2007 Bilbo got into serious trouble right here in Sennen. He and I would often walk out to Ayr Point, the far end of Gwynver beach, and then swim all the way to Sennen. It would take us about fifty minutes and Bilbo would go at about the same pace as me. I was never a really fast swimmer – I was quick enough, but I was never a competition swimmer. Anyway, on this particular day we were doing a training swim and because we had somebody else swimming with us – our friend George – we were swimming into the harbour, rather than through the surf into the beach, which was what we usually did.

With hindsight, I should have stayed a bit closer to Bilbo but I was swimming ahead as I normally did, because he would always catch me up. George had a pair of flippers on and he was swimming behind Bilbo, mucking about in the water. Suddenly he started screaming and shouting at me. I turned round and saw George waving his arms, so I raced back to where he was and found Bilbo all tangled up in some floating fishing ropes. He was completely tied up and the more he turned around in the water trying to get away from them, the more they wrapped round him. He whined and gasped and I could see he was in real distress. And, worse, he seemed to be sinking. He wouldn't have been getting waterlogged because of his special fur, but he was getting tired and the weight of the ropes was dragging him down.

I was desperately trying to hold him up in the water, treading water myself, but it was difficult because what could I do? I didn't have a knife and I couldn't bite through the ropes as they were over two centimetres thick. I felt absolutely awful as I should have been more aware of where he was heading and kept a proper eye on him, rather than leaving it up to George.

Mercifully, there was a drilling rig in the harbour. They were trying to make the bottom of the lifeboat slipway deeper, so they were drilling and blasting the rocks underneath the seabed there. Luckily one of the workers saw what was happening and came out in a rubber boat with a knife and managed to cut the ropes. It was quite an alarming ten minutes. I could hear Bilbo making a sort of whining sound. I could tell he was worried because he was trying to climb onto me. I didn't panic – thirty years of lifeguarding does have its benefits – I just kept talking to him, lovely and calm. 'You're a good boy, Billy,' I whispered. 'Yes, he's my good boy. Hold on, hold on. Soon be free,' I repeated while the chap and I hacked through the ropes. But it was such a shock, and a real lesson to me. I made sure I kept closer to him from then on.

Not long after that there was a basking shark that came into the harbour and it too got entangled in floating ropes and died. That was a warning that we took into schools – I'd tell the children to stay away from floating ropes and lobster pots in harbours, because even the best swimmer in the world can get caught up in them and drown.

There were other dangers too. It was around the same time, at Chapel Carn Brea, that Bilbo saw his first snake. It was a warm spring day and Bilbo was sniffing around up ahead when he suddenly froze. Stock still, he was staring at a spot about two metres away and there, rearing up in strike position, was a large adder, Britain's only poisonous snake. Even at a young age Bilbo recognized the signals of the wild, because he stopped still and didn't move. He seemed to know it wasn't a good idea to go for it. Luckily it was the time of year when the adders are lazy, and very slowly –

and with some soft encouragement from me, it has to be said – he backed away from the threat. The snake would have had a hard job getting through his fur, mind you, but it could have bitten him on the mouth.

15

VIP (Very Important Pet)

I always told the other lifeguards to be friendly and chatty on patrol, because in my experience it got you more respect than being aloof. And having Bilbo with us definitely made us more approachable. As Mark put it so eloquently: 'When you're a young lifeguard, you do a lot of fitness training and you get a bit buff. The sun comes out and you put bronzing time in and your sunnies on and go and talk to someone – and instantly they think you're full of it!' But when we started getting amongst people with Bilbo, the beach vibe changed. Once they knew our names, everyone would just chat a lot more.

Bilbo's cachet had come to the attention of big business and – like any supermodel worth their salt – he was signed up by a major company. Purina, the pet food manufacturer, was willing to pay us a small fee and keep him in dog food all year if he would become a member of their Dog Protection Team and attend Crufts in the March of 2007 as their guest. What's more, they would put the two of us up in a four-star hotel for the duration of the prestigious four-day show. They had actually first contacted us the previous year, but too late for him to go to Crufts.

I had always groomed Bilbo myself, washing him with warm water from a bucket while he stood there patiently as I checked his feet and ears – although he didn't like his feet being touched because they were very ticklish! But you have to cut the hair between the pads because if it gets too thick and matted it could cause a problem. They say you should always pay particular attention to a dog's feet – like a horse's they really need to be kept clean. The biggest challenge was getting him dry because his coat was so thick, so I got an industrial drier for him which I called the blaster. It had a long hose, like a vacuum cleaner, and was four horsepower! It was the only thing that would do the job and even with that it would take a good half-hour to dry him when he'd been in the sea.

While Bilbo was always well kept, I felt that a visit to the showground of the best of the best called for a professional touch. 'Billy,' I said to him, 'if you're going to attend the biggest dog show in the world, we'd better get you suited and booted!' And off we went to the dog groomers. Once there, the groomer sized him up with pursed lips and announced it would take at least an hour and a half to 'do' him. But when I went to pick him up she said, 'Oh, he was really easy, he was finished after forty minutes.'

Purina was the first company (after the Old Success Inn who had paid for his lifeguard jacket) to show interest in sponsoring Bilbo. Every year they had a team of dogs at Crufts whose job it was to protect people. There were fire dogs, bomb disposal dogs, hearing dogs and guide dogs. And because Bilbo was the only dog who was helping people on the beach they wanted him to join the team. In fact it became an event in our calendar for the next three years.

Each time we were put up at the Arden House Hotel, which is situated close to the show's venue, the National Exhibition Centre in Birmingham. We were due to leave Cornwall early in the morning for the long drive. I had packed everything into the 4x4 the night before and Bilbo, as usual, had noticed the goings-on. 'Don't worry, Billy, I'm not leaving you,' I reassured him. 'We're off on an adventure tomorrow.' He stuck to me like glue for the rest of that evening. He must have known that something special was in the offing as he had an extra-long grooming session. In the morning we had a long walk at first light and Bilbo even had a light breakfast. As we drove away from Chez Noir, he had his head out of the window, just having one look around before settling down with a full tummy on a very comfy bed. The journey took us seven hours in all as we had two stops to let both of us stretch our legs and have a drink. Bilbo found plenty of smells to investigate at the motorway services! It was mid to late afternoon when we pulled into the car park of our hotel. I was looking forward to checking in and relaxing but we had to do a tour of the hotel grounds first so Bilbo could do *his* checking in!

Reception was a hoot too when the staff realized they had a celebrity to stay. People even came from the kitchens to see him. Eventually we were settled in our room and I fed and watered Bilbo before I popped downstairs for some much needed refreshment. I walked into the hotel bar and people immediately went: 'Where's Bilbo?'

'Up in his room,' I said.

'Up in his room!' they cried. 'Well, don't leave him up there – bring him down here!'

I was a bit dubious because Bilbo was only three at the time. 'Well, OK . . . if you're sure,' I said. So I brought him down to the expensively decorated lounge, whereupon he proceeded to sniff at, then cock his leg against, one of the settees and peed all over it. But they didn't even mind! They just laughed and wiped it up. After all, Bilbo was a celebrity and trashing hotels is in the job description!

One thing for sure was that Bilbo knew how to make his presence felt; you could certainly say that for him. There was more embarrassment two years later when he met the BBC presenter Ben Fogle at Crufts, because I noticed later when I looked at a photograph of them together, that – how can I put this? – Bilbo had his lipstick out. Clearly he had taken a bit of a shine to Ben! However, when Bilbo was chosen as Dog of the Day on the working dogs' day he had to sit with Ben and his co-presenters Matt Baker, Clare Balding and *It's Me or the Dog* presenter Victoria Stilwell, and he was a model of good behaviour. He just lay demurely at Ben's feet, as good as gold, prompting Clare Balding to say that he was *definitely* their 'dog of the day'!

At Crufts we were on the Purina stand and that first year I was allocated quite a few slots to talk to the public. I would show a DVD of Bilbo on the beach, in the water, and doing mock rescues in the sea. There was always a great crowd of people standing around listening to our stories. We both enjoyed the experience, Bilbo especially as he just *loved* the attention. For my part it was an opportunity to spread the word of beach safety to a completely new audience.

Bilbo and I made new friends through Crufts. One woman came to the show just to see Bilbo and later told me that her life changed the day she met him. She fell in love with the breed and now has four Newfoundlands of her own. And she looks after cockatiels and other animals – not to mention a partner! I don't know how she manages it. She also worked part time in a monkey sanctuary then. She did loads for Bilbo and me, arranging for him to have his own business cards printed, as well as merchandise such as key rings and fridge magnets. She also helped me set up a website for him, bilbosays.com.

That summer we did a show for BBC1's *Animal Rescue Live* on the beach during the daytime. They were filming Bilbo rescuing Mark in the sea when the tide suddenly turned and we got called away from filming to help shepherd holidaymakers to another part of the beach. It actually worked out quite well for the TV crew because they used some of it in the show. I was in the water directing people, and Mark had a soaking wet Bilbo on the quad and was struggling to hold on to him; as we were doing hand signals to each other Bilbo was getting increasingly excited and agitated because he thought we were trying to call him into the water.

The show was a big hit for BBC Daytime, scoring great AIs – which is their Audience Appreciation index, indicating how much people like it. They had a solid audience of about a million viewers every day, apparently. On the back of that we were then asked to do a show for Battersea Dogs Home, and hardly a week went by when we weren't on *Animal Planet* on Sky. For that programme, Bilbo had to compete against one of our lifeguards, James, in a test to see which of them could rescue two 'casualties' from the sea in the shortest time. James was twenty-five, six feet tall and weighed eleven and a half stone. He could swim 4.2 kilometres an hour, meaning he was at optimum fitness for a lifeguard. Even so, my money was on the dog! Sure enough, James swam out to the people quicker than Bilbo managed to, and although Bilbo lost a bit of time swimming round the casualties before they caught hold of the Peterson tube, he caught up with James on the way in and just managed to pip him to the post. James was genuinely surprised to be beaten by Bilbo, who had towed in a combined twenty-four stone of human being with ease. But then, as I've said, a Newfoundland can tow a boat – they are that strong.

Bilbo might have looked the business on TV, but I wasn't exactly ready for my close-up. In fact, if you look carefully at that programme, I am missing one of my bottom teeth because Bilbo had knocked it out just moments before the crew arrived! When I lost my top teeth in the accident, it loosened some of the teeth on the bottom as well and when Bilbo and I were playing he jumped up and knocked one out. So I had to go on camera with this silly gap and try to talk without opening my mouth!

Once we had the website up and running, things just took off. Bilbo had his own Facebook page with five thousand followers, the maximum number allowed. Groups followed him as well. And because so many people wanted to know about him I decided to write the story of his life thus far. *The True Story of Bilbo the Surf Lifeguard Dog* was self-published in 2008. I wrote it with a locally based author who had already self-published and dedicated it to my mum, and to all the children of the world.

So many children were mad about Bilbo. They would even collect his fur off the beach when I groomed him. They wanted something to remember him by at the end of their holiday and the booklets were a good way of making them aware of beach safety at the same time. My daughter Kate put some in her coffee shop in Penzance because she said the tourists loved reading about Bilbo. She'd always tell the children that Bilbo was her brother! To date we have sold an incredible ten thousand copies.

We also made a DVD featuring Bilbo bounding into the sea like a lion or tiger. He loved being a surf dude, and looked the part as his chocolate-coloured fur became lighter as the sun and salt water bleached it until it was almost blond. If anything this only served to make him more handsome and garnered him further admirers! Come the winter, he would gradually change back to his original chocolate colour. He also gained weight when he was training in the summer months because he was building muscle from going up and down the dunes so often.

Mark, meanwhile, had become known locally as 'Bilbo's Professional Casualty' because he was always being rescued in the videos. He used to get mocked quite a lot, just friendly stick. His friends would say, 'Haven't you learnt not to go swimming, because that dog always has to come and save you!'

We would usually schedule any filming for our days off, otherwise the camera crews would have to come down really early in the morning because we obviously had work to do.

It seemed everyone wanted Bilbo on their television show. Paul O'Grady asked us to go on his programme and we would have loved to because of course he is a big dog lover. But we weren't allowed to in the end because we'd already appeared on *Richard & Judy*, who were the 'competition'. Richard and Judy were among the first to know about Bilbo because they live in Cornwall themselves, and we featured on their show the week after Bilbo did his first Newlyn to Penzance swim. We didn't go into the studio on that occasion; they sent a crew down and Bilbo was filmed 'rescuing' their researcher, Jo, from the sea. She acted the drowning damsel very well, I have to say!

We also featured on *The Sharon Osbourne Show*, along with fellow guest David Hasselhoff – yes, Mr Baywatch himself, and the man who, in my opinion, had single-handedly made us real lifeguards into a worldwide laughing stock! *Baywatch* didn't do us any favours at all, let me tell you. We spent years trying to live it down. Incidentally, he claimed to have met Bilbo before. He said: 'Oh, I saw that dog swimming around in the Thames.' But of course Bilbo had never been to the Thames. I don't know – what some people will do to try and ally themselves with the beautiful and famous! It's tragic . . .

By now Bilbo's fame was spreading far and wide. Bizarrely, he even featured in a French lads' mag called *Guts*, his picture appearing between the pages of scantily clad young women! Conversely, I was sent a photograph of a little girl from Nepal, who was proudly holding a copy of Bilbo's DVD. It turned out that some people from around our way had gone to Everest and taken copies of our DVD with them which they'd given out to the locals in Tibet.

Bilbo was a truly international pin-up. As well as writing fan mail people would send him gifts from all over the world. He got a cute bandana from a lady in Melbourne, Australia, who had seen him on TV and made it for him. It had koalas and emus and kookaburras on it. It just turned up one morning, addressed to 'Bilbo, Sennen Cove, Cornwall'. He was also presented with an appropriately huge pottery water bowl with his name on it, which was made for him by a very kind local potter.

We got all sorts. A young fan sent him one of her soft toys that she said she didn't like very much. It was Sylvester, the black and white cat who appeared with Tweetie Pie in the Looney Tunes cartoons, accompanied by a letter asking me to send her a photograph of Bilbo with his gift. Bilbo actually never played with toys; he didn't chase things either – he just wanted to be human. Even so, I did, of course, dutifully send the child a picture of him with the toy.

Bilbo was even given the use of his own private lake – a man-made lake in Sennen that he was given carte blanche to use whenever it was too rough for him to swim in the sea. It was about a hundred metres across and he used to go and swim down there all the time – he loved it. I would walk around the edge and throw things in for him. He would dive in and get them, but he wouldn't bring anything back because he wasn't a retriever.

Nor was Bilbo above the odd showbiz act of petulance. One time, *Pets at Home* came down to the beach and put all these bottles of dog beer in front of Bilbo for a promotion they were running. But Bilbo wouldn't drink it. I poured out one of each, and he just looked at me as if to say: 'I'm not drinking that!'

There were downsides to having such a well-known pet,

in that if he did anything wrong everyone knew immediately who he was. Worse, they knew who I was – and where I lived! Like the time I was walking Bilbo at Upton Towans, that huge stretch of beach at Hayle. At half-tide it is about two hundred metres from the water's edge to the cliffs and Bilbo and I were there one day when there was virtually nobody else on the beach. I saw this woman hollering and waving and she had a black and white dog with her. She obviously thought I was somebody else because she came running across the beach towards me, but when she was about a hundred metres away she realized that I wasn't who she thought I was and turned away and walked off.

Of course by this time Bilbo had already engaged with her shouting and waving and he thought: I'm going to go and find out what's going on. So he took off after her, and although I was shouting for him to come back he wouldn't. He was hell bent on getting to her dog so he could play with it. The woman had a stick which she was throwing for her dog. I had taught Bilbo that if I was holding something in my hand, and my hand was down by my side, he mustn't touch it; but if I waved it around in the air, then it was OK because it was a game. The woman must have got fed up with Bilbo getting the stick each time she threw it, so she was holding the stick above her head out of Bilbo's reach. But of course to his mind it was now 'Game On' and I could see him jumping up and down in the distance.

Anyway, she dropped the stick and bent down to pick it up. But she had a camera around her wrist and as she and Bilbo both went to get the stick, Bilbo's mouth crunched on her camera – although I didn't know that at the time. I was still calling him and he finally decided that he would come back and headed off towards me. By this time I could see that she was really angry about something but she didn't seem in the mood for talking.

Half an hour later, though, she turned up at the lifeguard depot. In the end, I agreed to replace her camera. It was one of those nifty little Canon compacts and cost me about a hundred and thirty quid. Plus she wanted the exact model, which they weren't selling anymore, so I had to scour eBay to try and find one. Bilbo also chewed an AC/DC box set that my mate Shaun lent me. I had left him in the car while I popped into the post office in Hayle, and when I came out there was shattered plastic all over the front seat. Cost me £30 to replace that too. He obviously liked AC/DC!

Such indiscretions aside, Bilbo was enveloped by love and goodwill everywhere he went. How many dogs, for instance, have their own birthday party? Not many, I'll bet. On 5 May 2008 Bilbo celebrated his fifth birthday in style. It was a couple of friends who came up with the idea. 'Let's have a birthday party for Bilbo!' they said one day in April. 'It'll be great fun.' I agreed, thinking it would be a good way to drum up interest in beach safety prior to the season starting in a couple of weeks at Whitsun. We asked our chums at the Old Success Inn if we could hold it there and they readily agreed.

One of the barmen lived on a large farm just outside Sennen village and we had a massive sign put up in one of the fields adjacent to the road, saying: 'Please come to Bilbo's Fifth Birthday Party at the Old Success Inn. Everyone welcome!'

On the day, which was lovely and sunny, three hundred

people came off the beach and from miles around to help him celebrate, which was amazing considering it was still out of season. The party started at eleven o'clock and went on until about three in the afternoon. Lots of people brought him presents – mainly bones and treats – and my friend's sister baked him a cake, which was really for the kids. Bilbo wasn't allowed any, to his disappointment I'm sure, because it was a chocolate cake. But he had balloons and lots of dog treats. Rowe's, the local bakery, donated all the savouries and pasties for the party. They brought boxes and boxes down; it was so kind of them.

Bilbo had a great time because he got fussed and given ice cream. We had people trying to give him beer, but I knew from bitter past experience that beer gave him the runs. Let's just leave it at that. Anyway, he was pretty wiped out afterwards from all the patting he'd received. Everyone was in a great mood that day, with the sun shining and the prospect of the holiday season just around the corner.

Little did we know, however, that it was to be one of the last happy days on the beach for Bilbo and me . . .

16

Hound Hailed As Hero

Since its inception in 1974, Penwith District Council had prided itself on having an excellent safety record on its manned beaches around Land's End. Further up the coast, the beaches in and around Newquay had benefitted from an up-and-running lifeguard service for some years, manned in the main by visiting Australians and holidaying surfers. Even in those days Newquay was fast becoming very popular as a West Country holiday resort, and people were increasingly willing to travel even further west to explore the coast.

Local surfers in West Penwith were already seeing the warning signs. The waves around Newquay and north Cornwall in general were becoming crowded as surfers were beginning to get the map out and discover our beaches. Suddenly Volkswagen camper vans were turning up in *our* car park, looking at *our* waves. It was a vibrant time and the local pubs were often quite lively! Lifeguards Jeff Devaney from Perth, Western Australia, Keith Millar from Wollongong, New South Wales, and Mark 'Wortho' Worthington were amongst the first lifeguards to work for the newly formed Penwith Council. All of them, despite being a long way from home and hardly qualifying as locals, were passionate about 'their' patch and 'their' waves. Like me, they were watermen, carrying on the tradition of lifeguards at Sennen, caring about the ocean and helping those who did not understand it. Perfect company for Bilbo when he joined the ranks later on.

The council's lifeguard service was a well-run oper-ation. It had to be when you consider we had fifteen beaches to cover, approximately sixty miles of coastline, and I think the staffing levels were fewer than forty lifeguards – even in the peak season. We were a small, tight-knit unit, and most of us were mates as well as colleagues. It was difficult to be taken on as a Penwith lifeguard in those days, espe-cially on the surf beaches. I always referred to us as the 'Legendary Penwith Lifeguards' because of our history and the characters that worked for us. We had – and maintained – high standards, believing in looking after our home turf, spectacularly beautiful west Cornwall.

I think this close-knit team was the reason we reduced the number of seasonal rescues from previous years' tallies of over one hundred per season to somewhere between forty and fifty. When Bilbo came along with his red and yellow jacket, spreading the word of beach safety far better than any sign, the rescues continued to fall – dramatically so in fact. However, a financial crisis was about to hit the British economy and local councils were having to make severe budget cuts. Suddenly, in 2008, our lifeguard service was under threat. It was then that a big company made the council an offer they simply could not refuse. Places like Porthcurno, Logan Rock, Sennen itself and Gwynver are truly special beaches; they really are, and so any company would be proud to manage them. Diving in the waters around here is incredible; the water is among the clearest in England. I used to do some salvage diving around Land's End, where it was as clear as gin and teeming with wildlife. I will never forget the patches of sea cliff that were colonized by a lone male crawfish, surrounded by countless hens! It was a fantastic sight to behold.

Of course change is inevitable, and things were changing within the lifeguard service. That's how I saw it, anyway. I feared it would soon be time to say goodbye. When I left the MOD and started working on the beach, it was to get away from the corporate world but nowadays, with health and safety laws, companies are required to have so many systems in place.

Lifeguarding for me was more of a way of life than a job. We often chose to work extra hours. For example, we weren't due at work until ten o'clock in the mornings, because that was the time that most holidaymakers would leave their campsite and head for the beaches. However, in reality, people started arriving as early as eight thirty, so Bilbo and I would get there early and just hang out, unofficially, to be on hand should anyone need us. In the case of someone who was perhaps making towards the rip, we would go down and head them off because – even with no flags on the beach – it was a good opportunity to explain the workings of the rip to them.

Times were changing and it seemed that Bilbo and I were spending less and less time on the beach. In Bilbo's case, this was because of council by-laws in place that enforce a dog ban on most beaches in the area in the summer.

Bilbo's core supporters launched a petition to try to get Bilbo's beach access reinstated. The response was overwhelming and within days it had an incredible twenty thousand signatures. A DVD called *Bilbo the Movie* was put together in which people were asked to help Bilbo by signing his petition. There was a campaign on Facebook and the national press inevitably got wind of the story. 'Britain's Lifeguard Dog Bilbo Banned from the Beach!' screamed the headlines.

We had so much support and eventually it was agreed that Bilbo could carry on his duties as long as they were educational. I was elated.

I missed having him there but, while I was down in the dumps, Bilbo did something really quite extraordinary which thrust him back into the media spotlight . . .

Bilbo and I were on our regular rounds checking the buoyancy aids at the more remote beaches and when we stopped at one of the coves close to Land's End I was surprised to see a woman walk past with a towel under her arm. There was a strong swell running that day, making it dangerous for anyone to go in the water, let alone swim safely. Earlier that day I had already told Bilbo off for trying to get into the water as the shore break came in.

I stopped and, turning around, said: 'Excuse me. You are not thinking of going for a swim are you?' Bilbo had also taken an interest by now and was sniffing at her towel, his big tail slowly swishing from side to side.

'Oh, ja,' she replied in a foreign accent. 'I am on holiday and swim here every day.'

'I don't think it's a good idea,' I said. 'The sea has changed since yesterday and it's not safe.' But – and I'm afraid this was not unusual – she ignored my advice and headed for the water's edge. Bearing in mind there was no safety cover on that beach, I tried to explain again how the conditions had changed and that today was not a good day for swimming. Maybe there was a language difficulty but she still ignored my advice. As she headed down onto the beach, I decided to keep an eye on her from where we were as we strolled slowly up the path. Bilbo, however, seemed very reluctant to go further and just stood there. 'Come *on*, Billy. We still have two more coves to visit,' I said to him. But he wasn't listening.

Then something amazing happened. Suddenly, and without any prompting from me, Bilbo took off and ran to the beach, full tilt at the woman who was now walking towards the sea wearing her bathing costume. He sped down the winding, uneven path, pushing past the thorny brush and through long grass to get to the beach. It only took him a couple of seconds to get there, and he ran across it, leaving clouds of sand and great big paw prints behind him.

Bilbo placed himself firmly between the woman and the sea, actually standing on her feet at one point. I could see and hear her gesticulating and shouting something.

I called and called for Bilbo to come to me but he just refused point blank. I now realized what he was doing – he was actually trying to prevent the woman from getting any-where near the water.

'Tell your dog to go away,' she shouted to me. But although I called him, Bilbo would not come. He was intent on stopping her getting in the sea. I had never seen him do anything like that before.

But the woman wasn't having any of it. She pushed her way past Bilbo and headed to the water, whereupon he raced into the surf to block her way. Only then did she realize how strong the current was, and as she saw what a difficult time Bilbo was having in the powerful waves she didn't go in.

The woman, who I later found out was a Dutch holiday-maker, told me she believed Bilbo saved her life that day. His actions in stopping her from getting into difficulty in the water made the local paper, bringing him yet more media attention.

'I thought he wanted to play at first,' she told reporters. 'He was walking in front of me, almost on my feet, and I had to push him aside. But then I realized he was trying to stop me going into the sea. When he realized he couldn't stop me he swam out quite far to show me how hard it was for him to get back. He didn't try to scare me – he didn't bark or anything.'

He had saved her life, not this time by barking, as with the little girl in the surf a couple of summers back, but by communicating through his actions. While a lifeguard will get involved in some seriously dramatic rescues in his time, we actually save far more lives by prevention. Bilbo proved time and time again that he could do just that.

I gave a quote to the newspapers in which I said: 'Bilbo is bigger than Lassie.' It was meant as a joke because Bilbo was physically bigger than a rough collie, but of course it was taken to mean that he was more famous than the legendary Lassie, and made Mark laugh, at least.

Laurence Reed, one of the presenters on BBC Radio

Cornwall, was also a fan of Bilbo's. He said on his programme: 'I really want to meet this dog, so if you're
listening, Bilbo, come up and see me tomorrow at the Royal
Cornwall Show.' Mark's girlfriend heard this and said to
Mark: 'We've got to take Bilbo to see him because no one
ever gets invited to meet Laurence Reed!' Suffice to say,
Laurence Reed, who was going to be presenting his programme from the event, is really popular with the listeners
because he's a bit cheeky and he likes to stir things up.

The Royal Cornwall Show is held every year in early
June at their showground in Wadebridge. It's a massive
agricultural show and Princess Anne usually attends. On
this occasion, however, the indomitable Princess Royal was
to find herself upstaged by Bilbo!

Mark regaled me with a full report that evening. As per
usual with anything involving Bilbo, things had not gone
according to plan. 'It was absolute chaos, J'mo,' he laughed,
clearly still feeling the buzz of the day's events. 'We walked
in the gates and I was trying to keep a low profile, thinking
that we'd just go and see Laurence Reed. He wasn't on until
about eleven o'clock and we got there at eight, thinking
we'd have a walk round the show. I thought I'd get myself
a bacon sandwich but it took until ten o'clock for us to walk
the forty yards to the stand because we were just mobbed
by swarms of kids!'

Bilbo didn't even have his lifeguard coat on because
Mark had thought – in a dastardly spot of cunning – that
he would take him disguised as an ordinary dog. Some
chance! Of course everyone recognized him.

'My girlfriend became impatient quite quickly because
we were held up by all the attention Bilbo was getting,'

Mark said. 'Not just from children – people of all ages wanted to see him, touch him, hug him, and have their photo taken with him. It was just crazy.' Mark didn't need to tell me. It was always the same when Bilbo went out in public. But however many people wanted to meet Bilbo, we always gave them the time. You couldn't ask for better behaviour from Bilbo either. He'd go into what Mark called his 'statue mode' – to the point where kids would be shoving ice cream into his face and he wouldn't even lick it. You could tell he wanted it because there was ectoplasm-like drool coming off him, but as far as Bilbo was concerned he was at work and knew what was required of him. That was Bilbo all over. He was so placid he just won everyone's heart.

17

A Bilbo-Shaped Hole

That autumn, my mum became ill. She was eighty-two and had been in reasonable health up until then. But her next-door neighbour, Ruth, called me one morning in October 2008 to say she had been admitted to hospital the previous evening. She was in the Gilbert Bain hospital in Lerwick, suffering from water retention caused by heart failure and the onset of kidney trouble. The doctors were saying that she might have to have dialysis, and it was clear they were very worried about her.

Although I was only able to see her once a year because of the distance, I was really close to my mum and flew straight up there when I got the call. When I arrived at the hospital she was very poorly. In fact, I walked straight past her bed because I didn't even recognize her. I had to go back to reception and say, 'Where's Nell Jamieson?' They pointed her out and I just thought: Flipping heck. Everything about her had changed. She'd aged massively. She always used to look after her hair – she wore it in this bouffant style and was considered very glamorous – but now it was white and straight. She looked completely different.

She was so poorly the doctors warned me that she might not survive. But I just refused even to contemplate it. I asked her: 'What are you eating in here, Mum?' Because by the look of her she was eating very little. Much of the time when I was growing up it had been just the two of us, because Dad was away such a lot. Mum taught me every-thing – how to cook, sew, darn, knit – so I was able to look after myself when I left home. And now I had the opportun-ity to look after her. I knew that she loved lentil soup so I made her some each day and took it to the hospital. I would go up there at eleven o'clock in the morning and stay with her until seven in the evening. I also made healthy stews, which I liquidized, and would sit and feed them to her and make sure that she ate properly every day.

Mark had Bilbo for me. It was a big ask because it wasn't easy looking after him. If they took care of Bilbo for even one day, most people would say, 'That was nice but you can have him back now.' Whereas it was a minimum of ten days or a fortnight when I went to Shetland for my annual visit, and longer when Mum was ill.

In the event, I was up there for nearly a month. My priority was getting Mum well again. I concentrated all my efforts into feeding her up, to the point where – to their surprise because they could hardly believe it – the hospital said she was well enough to go home. I'd been up in Shet-land to see her the year before and noticed that she couldn't get up and down the stairs very easily, so I'd brought her bed downstairs and made it up for her in the front room so she could continue to stay at home rather than go into residential care. Alterations had been made to the house for Dad when he was due to come out of hospital, which he never did. The council had put a special toilet and shower downstairs for him, so Mum had those, and her kitchen – and of course her lifelong neighbours next door.

She was looking much better and by the time I left Shetland and headed home, I felt confident about leaving her. I organized a care package for her, and social services in Shetland were really quite good. She had someone coming in to help her with her meals and so forth, so I knew she would be all right.

I'd missed Bilbo massively of course. I'd hated being without him. It had been almost five weeks since I had dropped him off at Mark's and I was very excited at the prospect of seeing him again. As I arrived, Mark opened the door and there Bilbo was, looking magnificent. 'Quality grooming, Mark,' I said, impressed.

'Aye, aye, Captain. Only the best for the King,' came the reply as Bilbo, his face all scrunched up, barged past Mark. His tail was going mad, batting everything near him. 'Steady on, Billy,' said Mark. 'You'll shake yourself over in a minute!'

He was so pleased to see our 4x4 standing there, door open, he sprang straight in!

Driving back to Chez Noir, Bilbo took up his normal position between the front seats, but today he was almost *in* the front with me. I had to stop the car at one point and rearrange him. 'That's a bit enthusiastic, Billy,' I said, but the response I got was a cold stare!

'And you can stop that too, my lad,' I said sternly, climbing back into the front.

For the rest of that day, he was what I would call grumpy with me, to the point where, when we were having a play-fight, he nipped me on the arm as if to say, 'Well, that's for leaving me behind!'

Mark had told me that the first time Bilbo stayed with him and his girlfriend she was pleased and excited to have him, but the novelty quickly wore off because she didn't like the way he smelled. Bloody cheek! Bilbo always smelled wonderful (if you like the smell of wet dog, that is). So the first day he arrived he had to go straight into the bath, followed by a thorough grooming session. We'd been given some dog deodorant at a dog show and when that ran out he was bought some coconut deodorant. After every walk Mark had to wash him and dry him and deodorize him in order to keep her happy.

But what she did love about having him to stay was playing hide and seek with him. 'We'd leave Bilbo downstairs, turn off all the lights in the house – so there was just a bit of moonlight or streetlight coming through the window – and we'd tell him to "Stay" while we ran upstairs and hid,' Mark explained. 'What was hilarious was we could hear him clomping around, and we'd hide under the bed or behind the door, and he'd walk into each room and hold his breath while he listened for us. We'd be holding our noses or biting our arms just to stay quiet but neither of us could outlast him and we would always crack up. We'd wet ourselves laughing. We played that pretty much every night, just before bedtime. Bilbo loved it.'

It had been the same when he and I played hide and seek at the depot in St Ives when he was a puppy.

Mark's girlfriend's mum had a collie called Maggie, and

they often used to walk the dogs together. It was the same time every year, when I went back to Shetland, so it became a routine. Mark always insisted it was no trouble for him having Bilbo because he was 'one of the boys' and you could take him anywhere, but after he'd stayed with them a few times, coupled with the fact that Bilbo didn't usually pay much attention to women, his girlfriend began to find fault with him. 'He doesn't do the things with me that he does with you,' she'd complain to Mark.

Bilbo messed up big time when she was getting ready for an important business meeting. She had been a lifeguard and was into surfing when Mark met her, but she had a career change and started going to work in suits. She had bought a new dress and jacket to wear to London, had spent ages getting ready and was just about to head off and drive up there. 'I was downstairs with Bilbo and she came down and said to me, "Do I look all right?"' said Mark. 'But just then Bilbo shook his head and a bit of drool flew across the room and landed on her jacket and the dress.'

And, as I knew only too well, Bilbo's slobber was like glue; you couldn't sponge it off. He only 'dripped' if he was eating or drinking, but if he didn't drool for a while, the next time it appeared it had become really thick and sticky. I used to walk through Chez Noir sometimes and think: What the hell's that? And there would be this thing hanging on the wall, which upon closer inspection turned out to be a string of Bilbo's slobber.

'Well, she tried to wash it off but it left a stain so she just freaked out and went and got changed into her old suit,' said Mark. 'She went mental, which I thought was a bit over the top really. But Bilbo and I were both laughing. He looked like he had a smile on his face, anyway!'

Another thing that used to wind her up was when she cooked lasagne. Mark said it was as if Bilbo knew what the ingredients were in the bag before she'd even started cooking them. He'd just sit at the kitchen door waiting, as if he knew what was going to be coming out, whereas with other food he didn't bother. I know they used to give him a little bit because lasagne was always his favourite.

He wasn't averse to stealing a kid's ice cream either if the child was not 'on the case'. He would await his opportunity and then just have it! But because the children were so enamoured of Bilbo it didn't really matter. In fact I think they quite liked it if he ate their ice cream because usually their parents would then buy them another one. Certainly a lot of them would instinctively drop theirs when Bilbo came up to them.

Bilbo meant an awful lot to some people. There was a young girl from Penzance called Rosie, who had been diagnosed with a rare form of cancer. Her parents used to bring her to the lifeguard hut to visit Bilbo because she adored him. When she got really ill she said to her mum that the only thing she wanted to do was to see Bilbo so they put her in the car, drove to Sennen and parked in the car park, but she was too ill to make it out to the hut. They compromised by telling her they would go to the hut and take a photograph of Bilbo and bring it back to show her but Mark had Bilbo at the hut that day and as soon as they told him what was happening he walked Bilbo over to the car park so Rosie could see him.

She had been sick all morning and had a little tube in

her nose and no hair because of the chemotherapy she'd had but she lit up when she saw Bilbo. Bilbo tried to get in the car with her and she just sat with him, stroking him and smiling. That was the last time she saw him and the last time she came out of her house. Very sadly, she passed away in January 2010 aged sixteen.

Bilbo was mostly concerned with where his next meal was coming from, and whether there were any female dogs in the area who might appreciate a visit from Bilbo the Love God. We didn't have neighbours as such – the nearest house belonged to John and Gina, about eight hundred metres away. They had a beautiful flat-coated retriever bitch called Ruby and, like I say, Bilbo had a good nose for sniffing out girl dogs on heat. We were due west from this house and the wind had been blowing from the east on this particular day, and Bilbo had been enthusiastically sniffing the air all afternoon.

That evening he was tied up by his long rope outside Chez Noir and was making quite a racket – if love was in the air sometimes he would howl as well. I was thinking: Oh, it's going to be one of those nights, is it? I guessed he was desperate to go and see Ruby, so I brought him inside and shut the door and locked it, not just with the key but bolted it too.

Chez Noir was very old and pretty ramshackle and I knew he could get onto the cooker and open the window. It only had a simple latch holding it closed and Bilbo had seen me open it many times to let the steam out when I was cooking. He was pretty smart like that; he'd watch and learn and he'd been out of that window a few times. So that evening I got a screwdriver and screwed the window into itself so it couldn't be opened. I went to bed and was out like a light until I was awoken at five in the morning by my phone ringing. It was Gina. 'Steve, he's in the garden!' she said. 'What? He can't be!' I replied sleepily, remembering how I had locked the door and window. But when I stumbled bleary-eyed into the kitchen and stared into the gloom: lo and behold – it was as if Dan Dare had gone through the door! Literally, *through* it. There was a dog-shaped hole in the door and splinters of wood on the ground outside.

I went out and got him, which I wasn't too pleased about at that time of the morning. When I arrived, although I knew he was there somewhere, *he* also knew damn well that I was there looking for him and kept lurking in the dawn light's shadows, playing his 'hide and seek' routine to the limit. However, this day I just knew he was there somewhere so the game was up. As we walked back to Chez Noir, I said to him, smiling to myself, 'Good effort, Billy. Good boy.'

I knew of some people who bought electric collars for their dogs to stop them from running away, the ones where the animal gets a small electric shock if they try to leave the garden. And they do work – most dogs don't even have to wear the collars after a while because they've learnt not to cross the perimeter. I considered getting one for Bilbo, but I thought: No, it's down to me to know what he's doing. Even so my neighbour Leroy must have lost count of the number of times he saw me running up and down the lane shouting, 'Bilbo!'

But Leroy knew what Bilbo was like. There was the time I'd gone to the pub with Leroy and a couple of mates and I'd looped Bilbo's lead around the table leg. Bilbo had a tendency to lurch – because, like I say, he was capable of moving pretty quickly when he wanted to. That day he decided to get up and go and investigate something, taking the entire table with him! It shot about three metres across the pub and smashed our glasses, spilling drink everywhere. I was so embarrassed because there were all these tourists looking round as if to say, 'What's happened here?' Bilbo didn't even seem to notice the mayhem he'd caused but at least Leroy thought it was highly amusing!

He also never minded when Bilbo knocked him off his feet – which he did on a number of occasions. Leroy was coming over to Chez Noir one evening for a beer and I'd said, 'Bilbo's outside, just make sure you call him first so he knows you're coming.' So he came wandering round in the pitch dark, having forgotten his torch, and said, 'Bilbo, it's Leroy!' All he recalled after that was the sound of thundering hooves, and then a brief moment of silence before two huge paws hit him on the shoulders and he hit the deck. 'It was a bit like being rugby-tackled,' he said, good-naturedly. 'Bilbo was all slobbery and I was covered in mud – it was absolutely brilliant!'

Leroy's toddler daughter Molly absolutely adored Bilbo too. He was bigger than her, of course, but she would wander up and have a little stroke with him. It was lovely. I never had to worry about Bilbo with young kids because he was so good with them. They'd just climb all over him. Most dogs would get annoyed by it, but he was just chilled. My son Charlie's little girl Holly was particularly close to Bilbo and when she was three she used to lie on the floor with him, head to head. It was really sweet to see. Alice's kids, being younger, were a bit scared of him – but then they did not have any pets of their own and, let's face it, he towered above them. Bilbo knew to leave them alone, though. Kate said it was because he couldn't be bothered. She always said: 'Unless you're drowning, he ain't interested!'

Another time Bilbo ran nearly two miles back from Nanjulian to Gina's house because he wanted to get to Ruby. He'd been sniffing the air for a while and just took off. I could see him running along the coastal path and I was shouting until I was blue in the face. Every so often he'd stop and look at me, and then run off again, the blighter! I knew full well he was after a dog, probably Gina's, but there was another bitch that lived on a farm in Nanjulian so I had to go there first, to make sure he wasn't there. By the time I got to Gina's I was knackered because I'd done a five-mile run! For her part, Gina was worried her greenhouse was about to fall over because Bilbo was rushing around in such a frenzy!

We both thought Ruby and Bilbo would have made lovely puppies, though, and I did wonder if he had actually got to her, but he hadn't. Despite his best efforts to find a mate I don't think he has any progeny.

He had a great doggy friend called Hugo. I used to house-sit for Hugo and Megan, two springer spaniels, and after Megan died Hugo and Bilbo became real pals and used to go around together in the car (I'd be driving, I hasten to add!). It was quite amusing as Hugo – who unless he was travelling in the front was prone to car sickness – always had the front seat. Bilbo would sit as close behind me as he possibly could and rest his head on my shoulder, keeping a watchful eye on Hugo!

When I first got Bilbo a lot of people had suggested that I should get him neutered. They'd say things like, 'He'll get really aggressive when he's older if you don't.' But I just thought: Not if I have anything to do with it, he won't. And he didn't.

18

Six Weeks of Separation

The despair I felt at Mum being so poorly began to have an effect on my general well-being. In the end, I went to see my GP and she signed me off with stress for twelve months in all.

It was at this time that Bilbo and I began to look for new walks, more secluded ones especially. One time I was wondering where to go and remembered a fairly long walk around a local reservoir. It is a well-established reservoir that supplied the main town of Penzance with drinking water and is now teeming with wildlife and a popular angling spot to boot. Good plan, I thought, estimating that it would probably take about one hour max. We climbed into the 4x4, pushed it into gear, and drove out onto the main road towards Penzance.

As we arrived I noted it was about three o'clock in the afternoon. Great, plenty of time for a walk, I thought with a smile. Bilbo was already full of beans, realizing we had come to some place new. I could hear his great tail batting the inside of the car. Locking up the motor, we crossed over on top of the dam wall. Bilbo was being extremely inquisitive as usual, continually peering over the edge at the drop, not entirely sure what to make of it. Eager to push on, he was straining at the lead, keen to reach the shrubs and trees ahead. As we walked along the bank I could see that the water level was much lower than normal. By now, Bilbo was squealing with excitement as he had spied an easy entry point into the water. I had a quick scan around to see if there were any anglers nearby and, seeing none, let him loose. Seconds later, he was in his aquatic element – Bilbo heaven. I could see there were no other dogs in sight so I pushed on, further up the reservoir, him running free behind me. At the very end of the reservoir, I could see just how much the water had receded due to the drought of the past couple of years. There were even the walls of an old, long-submerged cottage showing out of the mud.

THE MUD! Aaaargh! I looked on in horror as Bilbo lolloped across the dry, crusted mud at the edge of the water and – *thwop!* – laid his huge body down in the wet gloop. There he stayed, like a hairy water buffalo, stuck fast in the mud. I could see his pathetic face looking at me as if to say: 'Here's another fine mess you've got me into!'

Although quite amusing to begin with, it soon became evident that Bilbo really *was* stuck. He was floundering about, trying to heave himself out, but by doing so was simply making things worse. I grabbed the only thing I could see in the vicinity, a long branch, and crept down towards him as far as I dared. Then I advanced just a little bit more, and a bit more still, until – you guessed it! – I got sucked into the boot-enveloping mud too! I was at least now close enough to Bilbo to be able to calm him down, and he looked a sorry picture, I can tell you, every inch of him covered in mud. Slowly but surely, and with gentle coaxing from me, I managed to get him to the point where he could cling to the branch I was stretching out in his direction and he eased himself bit by bit out of the ooze with his big webbed feet. Finally he was up and onto the hard crust, where he stopped and looked back at me, as if to say: 'Well, come on then, hurry up!'

But I was stuck in the mud myself, the branch was broken in three, and I was already minus a sock – not to mention being completely covered in sticky mud. Thankfully, bits of branch are better than none at all and I eventually managed to clamber out. All these time-consuming events, combined with the end of British Summer Time, meant that by now it was beginning to get dark. As I had been so preoccupied with rescuing Bilbo I had failed to notice the cooling mist that was slowly but steadily enveloping everything. What I did notice, however, was the fact that I did not have a coat and a fine drizzle was coming down. Grrr! I thought, looking at Bilbo resentfully. We set off at a sharp pace, but even so, it was pretty much dark by the time we arrived back at the car. I was cold, wet, and totally fed up with new walks!

All in all, 2009 was a grim year. Apart from a brief interlude in March, when Bilbo and I made our annual trip to Crufts, it was pretty much wall-to-wall gloom and doom as I struggled to cope with my low mood. I didn't even find our time at the show particularly enjoyable, to be honest, because I was feeling so exhausted. My mum was ill again and so far away, and I was anxious about the future. I was mildly cheered when the judges chose Bilbo as their Dog of the Day on the working dogs' day, but my worries were at the forefront of my mind.

Then to cap it all, just before Christmas Mum died.

Her health had steadily got worse so they had taken her into hospital. But, you know, it was actually kind of *all right* in the end, the way she went. The doctor rang me at ten o'clock in the evening ten days before Christmas. He had gone to give her some medication and had got her to sit up in bed because he was going to give her an injection. He'd asked her how she was feeling and Mum had said, 'I'm feeling really good because Steven's coming up on Thursday and I'm really looking forward to seeing him.'

The doctor said he turned round to get something from his tray and when he turned back again she was dead. I was comforted by the idea that when she died she was thinking about me. That was good.

At the time, Bilbo and I were house-sitting at his doggy friend Hugo's on the south coast. Bilbo loved it over there with Hugo as the garden was vast and teeming with rabbits. They had been having such fun.

That night we sat together in the darkness, Bilbo and I, for hours. I could not believe my mum was gone. Most evenings Bilbo would pad around until he had checked out all the rooms, before settling down for the night, but he did not move from my side that evening. In fact, every now and again he would sit up and put his massive paw on me and, looking up with those eyes – those big pools of amber – he was saying, 'I'm here, it's OK, Captain.'

We then had a fuss and the contact took my mind off things for a while. That night, instead of adopting his usual sleeping position by the front door, Bilbo slept lying across the door space to the room I was sleeping in. It was such a comforting sight to see him when I awoke the next morning.

I was in shock. Suddenly everything seemed almost surreal. I had already decided to go to Shetland to see Mum long before she was admitted to hospital. My flight was booked for 17 December and part of me had been dreading going up there, because I knew in the back of my mind that it was probably going to be the last time I would see her. And that would have been a terrible thing to have had to do: to say goodbye to her, knowing that I wouldn't see her alive again. So at least I was spared that.

I arranged everything by phone. I flew up on the Thursday, as planned, went to the hospital and got her death certificate and everything sorted out at the funeral parlour. I buried her on the Saturday, and flew back on Monday. I just locked up her house and left it because I couldn't face clearing it out at that point. I knew that once the house was empty and I shut the door and handed over the keys, I would not have anything to go back to.

The local council were brilliant. They just said, 'Don't worry, take as long as you need.' I went back to Shetland in February, and in the end I was up there for about six weeks. My cousin Gail came to help me sort everything out, and my daughter Alice flew up for a week as well to offer support, because for me to have to go and empty my mum's house was absolutely heartbreaking. I realized I don't want my kids going through any of that, so I'm going to get rid of my clutter a bit at a time. It makes you feel better anyway, I think; we don't really need all this stuff.

Bilbo stayed with Mark, who was now working as a lecturer at Falmouth University. He obviously couldn't take Bilbo to work with him at his new job so he used to drop him at his mum's house in Penzance in the morning.

But she was always a little bit wary of Bilbo on account of his size. One day while he was teaching, the college receptionist came in and pulled him out of his lesson. 'Your mum is on the phone and says that she really needs to talk to you,' she whispered. 'I don't know if it's an emergency or not.'

Mark's mum had never phoned him at work before, so of course he was wondering what had happened. He thought that maybe she'd lost Bilbo and was getting ready to say, 'I told you not to let him out!' We all knew by now that he would run away if he got the chance and wanted to go and investigate something. But when Mark got to the phone his mum said she couldn't get Bilbo to move away from the door, and as a result she was trapped in her own front room! He always liked to lie by the door – I think he liked the draught, and also that way he knew he wouldn't miss anything. Mark's mum had been asking him to move but, like I've said, Bilbo didn't really listen to women – he was used to men.

'It's easy, Mum, just ask him to get up,' Mark told her, exasperated at being taken away from his class. But she said she was too scared to and so she ended up putting the phone to Bilbo's ear while Mark shouted down it: 'Bilbo, get up!' He recognized his voice and jumped up straight away! Unsurprisingly, I think she preferred him to stay outside after that. Mark said she was cooking a roast dinner one Sunday and Bilbo was outside in the yard with his face pushed up against the glass door, drool running down the window.

Mark had bought his girlfriend a horse, a three-year-old shire cross thoroughbred called Molly-Molly who grew to be over sixteen hands. Bilbo used to like going down to the livery – probably because the horse was more his size! They used to sniff each other. Mark was worried Bilbo would get kicked so they kept him on the lead to begin with, but eventually all the horses got used to him. He was a model citizen at the livery, so nobody minded him being there. He loved drinking from the hosepipe in the yard. Mark's girl-friend would be hosing the horse down, and Bilbo would be merrily drinking from the end like a straw – a trait pecu-liar to many dogs, and in particular the Newfoundland.

That February it snowed heavily and they took lots of pictures of him for me, which was really thoughtful because I was missing him terribly. They took him to see the horse and there is a photo of the horse rolling around in the snow, with Bilbo standing in the background. And another, of *Bilbo* rolling around in the snow and the *horse* standing in the background! It reminded me of the first time Bilbo saw snow. It must have been about 2006 because he was still quite young and he couldn't believe this white stuff that was right outside his door. He ran out and lay down in it and made a Bilbo-shaped snow angel! Then he got up and started dashing around in it like a lunatic, but the snow compacted between his pads and turned to ice and I had to get it out for him.

Those six weeks I was in Shetland were the longest we'd ever been separated. I really hated being without him, and I don't think he was too happy about it either because the day I got back he once again gave me a nip on my arm, as if to say, 'Don't do that again.'

Everything was mounting up and I was not in a good place. It wasn't just Mum dying that was upsetting; it was also that while I was going through Mum's papers I found an old family tree that my uncle had begun. According to that, I'd had *three* siblings who had died, not two. I don't know where he or she came in the order of things, I don't even know their name. Mum and Dad never mentioned them to me, although Mum must have told me about Susan, the baby who never came home, otherwise I wouldn't have known her name.

It all unsettled me, and combined with losing Mum and having to leave Shetland I felt really low. Shetlanders are fiercely proud people and although I hadn't lived there for years it was my birthplace. Locking the door and leaving Shetland for the last time was just awful. It will always be where my roots are. It can never be the same but it will be good to see the 'Old Rock' again one day.

19

Bilbo in the Big Smoke

Thank goodness for Bilbo, because he was the only good thing in my life at that time. Losing my mum had knocked the stuffing out of me, quite frankly. I couldn't expect anybody to understand, but Shetland was a huge part of my life and Mum dying and having to leave there was dreadful. Bilbo really was my saviour. If it hadn't been for him, I wouldn't have known how to carry on.

I don't think I would have got out of bed in the morning and I would probably have ended up drinking a lot more. But, as it was, I had to feed him and walk him and deal with him every day. Bilbo was now seven years old but continued to require a lot of handling, as he was still very fit and extremely strong. With more time on my hands, our days inevitably became even more focused on each other.

And it's hard to be down all the time when you've got a dog because they live in the moment. Bilbo always brought a smile to people's faces – even my miserable mug! We used to go to the First And Last, which was our local pub in Sennen, and when there was a band playing the girls would get Bilbo up on the dance floor. They'd be dancing round him and he'd just stand there wagging his tail, looking for food. So maybe he was a chick magnet after all! Mind you, with the first glimpse of any drool most girls would usually shriek: 'Get him away from me!'

Bilbo was the recipient of lots of awards from Cornwall Animal Hospital because we used to go to see them at Redruth and support their dog shows and fundraising events. He got a little statue from them and several certificates for the work he did helping animal causes in the county.

Knowing that what we were doing was appreciated made me feel less disillusioned, for sure, and I was over the moon to be contacted in the summer of 2010 by the kids' television channel Boomerang and told that Bilbo had been nominated as their National Pet Hero of the Year. They had carried out a nationwide search to find the most 'talented, heroic and loveable pets in the UK' and Bilbo had been selected because of his courage bounding into the sea to rescue people, as well as the 'outstanding' work he and I did in the local community and schools.

He was on a shortlist of eight pets from various regions of the country and, as finalists, we were invited to London to attend the awards ceremony and the Boomerang Pets Party in Regent's Park afterwards. It was an all-expenses-paid trip and we were put up for three nights in some style at the Cannizaro House Hotel in Wimbledon. It was a fantastic place – full of footballers at the time, I seem to recall. The house had been a major social centre for royalty and senior politicians in its day, and King George III and Prime Minister William Pitt the Younger both stayed there regularly. Other famous guests were Lord Tennyson, Oscar

Wilde and the last Maharajah of the Punjab – and now Bilbo!

We stayed in the William Pitt Suite, which was one of the hotel's best and overlooked the park. There were three rooms in all: one for me, one for Bilbo, and a separate sitting room. There were two king-sized beds, a large bathroom with underfloor heating and a separate walk-in shower. There was even a television in the bathroom. We were there three nights and it was something like £670 a night. It was brilliant. They asked me: 'Tell us, what would Bilbo like for breakfast?' I said, 'Well, he's got his own food.' And they said, 'Yes, but he's on holiday, isn't he?' I said, 'Well, he likes sausages.'

The next morning there was a knock at the door and the waiter wheeled in this trolley which had two plates covered by silver butler's domes. The waiter removed these with a theatrical flourish and underneath one was my breakfast and in the other a plate of bacon and sausages for Bilbo! So he did really well staying there because they made such a big fuss of him. He didn't actually sleep in his king-size, I should hasten to add, as I always took his own bed with us wherever we went.

We wanted for nothing and there were taxis on tap if we needed to go anywhere. To top it all off, on the day of the awards ceremony in Regent's Park, Bilbo scooped first prize and was named 'Boomerang National Pet Hero of the Year 2010'. Announcing that Bilbo was their overall winner, Sally Bezant, spokesperson for the Boomerang Pets Party, said: 'Bilbo is one of a kind: a loving animal who is committed to saving lives and keeping kids safe. As soon as we heard Bilbo's tale we knew he was something special and we're truly delighted to be able to present this award to Bilbo today.'

By the following month his website had received over 60,000 hits. The VIP (very important pet!) was presented with his award by TV presenter Michaela Strachan and afterwards we were driven to the BBC studios, where we did a question and answer session with her. The cab took us right to the door and we were whisked in like true celebrities! We were connected to radio stations all over the country; we spoke to Radio Cornwall and Radio Newcastle amongst others. It was one after the other.

During the summer, Bilbo once again took part in the Newlyn to Penzance Swim, getting another medal to add to his growing collection! He also appeared as a guest at Newlyn Raft Day. The Pet Hero of the Year was then invited to London's biggest dog show, Discover Dogs, which was held every autumn at Earls Court. Bilbo was by now endorsing a Canadian holistic pet food company called Orijen, and we attended the show as their guest.

But in October that year Hugo, Bilbo's best doggy friend, passed away from old age. As I've mentioned, Bilbo wasn't terribly keen on other dogs because he wasn't socialized much as a puppy. His take on them was rather like his reaction to that kid in the fluffy suit he'd knocked over on the beach that day in Sennen. He would go bounding up to them, and of course nine times out of ten the first thing he would get from the other dog would be a bite. So he became very wary of small dogs and other unneutered males – huskies in particular. He was attacked by a husky when he was about eighteen months old and never forgot it. Maybe it was because their eyes were so close together and they seemed to stare so much. There was also a Hungarian Vizsla who had the same effect on Bilbo.

Every year, just before Christmas, the good people of Newlyn choose a celebrity or local dignitary to have the honour of switching on the harbour lights. It is usually someone like the mayor, or if any television shows are filming in the area – which they often are – they might ask an actor to do it. And that year I was really proud when they asked if Bilbo would come and switch on the Christmas lights. You have to give some kind of little address to the crowd – say what a great honour it is to turn these lights on, etc. So I prepared a speech along the lines of how it was really good for Bilbo to do it because of his connection with the people of Newlyn and the fishing industry. He loved the smell of Newlyn harbour and especially eating the fish. Oh, how Bilbo loved fish!

Bilbo and I stood on a veranda above the harbour-master's office and as I began my speech – thanking the organizers for inviting us, saying what a great honour it was, and talking about Bilbo loving the sea – I heard this voice out of the crowd below shouting, "Ere! That's my mate up there!' It was this fisherman we knew, who seemed a little worse for wear and was bullishly pushing his way through the spectators and trying to climb up the steps to see Bilbo.

There was a large pressure switch on the veranda and the plan was that Bilbo (but in reality me) would push the switch at the end of the speech, which would turn a light on underneath the veranda. That illuminated light would be the signal for the guys at the end of the harbour to let off the fireworks. Anyway, this fisherman was trying to make his way up the steps and people were trying to stop him. But I knew he just wanted a laugh so I said: 'It's all right, just let him up.'

So up he comes, saying, "Ere – Bilbo!' And of course Bilbo got excited, reared up at the guy, missed, and his paw landed on the pressure pad, which turned the light on. The next thing we know all the fireworks were exploding prematurely, before I'd even finished my speech! Everyone was like, 'For God's sake, what's going on?' But they all took it in good spirits!

Bilbo, meanwhile, was totally unfazed by all the commotion – including the fireworks. When he was a puppy I knew that it would be good for him to experience things like the noise of the rescue helicopter taking off, or an artic lorry releasing its air brakes; I burst balloons behind him – all that sort of thing. I had an inkling, even in those early days, that we could use him on the beach and I wanted him to be a stable dog. It worked, because if there were any loud bangs or fireworks, he would just look up, mildly interested, and then go back to sleep.

20

End of an Era

Inevitably, the old days were gone, and I decided it was time for me to move on. I was also still suffering from the loss of my mum and having to say goodbye to Shetland. In January 2011 I decided to leave the service. In reality, I hadn't been really involved on the beach for some time anyway. I had always known that the day would come eventually but I also knew it would take me a long time to come to terms with the change. It was the end of an era.

I started making jewellery and that summer we did some fundraising work for Cornwall Air Ambulance at the Royal Cornwall Show. I also decided to set up my own company, Bilbo Lifeguard Dog Community Interest Company Limited, and Bilbo and I resumed our beach safety classes in local schools. We stopped those for the year and a bit I had been off sick and we were both glad to get back into the classrooms again. We would usually be at a school for around two hours but of course that was only part of the job. I had to walk Bilbo and spend an hour grooming him before we were ready to leave, as I always wanted him to look nice for people. Then we might drive for up to an hour, as some of the schools we visited were in the north of the county. Sometimes we might do two schools in a day, so it could actually be quite a long day.

We would both be tired afterwards; me from all the driving and talking and Bilbo from all the petting and attention he'd received from the kids! We also started to visit old folks' homes, because people of all ages loved Bilbo. We'd go anywhere that he could cheer people up. And they really appreciated it. One elderly lady, who lived in a nursing home, wrote to ask me for a poster of Bilbo to put up in the communal sitting room because all the residents admired him so much. She wrote: 'He brightens everyone's day,' which was just lovely to hear.

We also had requests to attend shows all over Cornwall. Among the many charities and events we supported, one of our favourites was the National Mission to Deep Sea Fishermen. Not only did it provide a facility to help fishermen and their families, it was also an integral part of the social life of Newlyn port. Bilbo was always made extremely welcome by the staff whenever we visited. Each year the mission supported what has now become an established annual fixture, the Newlyn Fish Festival, a one-day event in and around the harbour area with plenty of stalls. A percentage of the takings is donated to supporting the mission. Bilbo was invited to set up his own stall on the harbourside, next to the mission itself – the only dog allowed inside the harbour area. A real privilege.

It was a great platform for us to promote his merchandise, as well as spread the word about beach safety. We would have his book, DVD, fridge magnets and stickers on sale, but trying to sell things at the same time as dealing with the many people who wanted to have their photo taken with Bilbo was nigh on impossible, so sales were never that lucrative for us. It was also a very long day, especially for Bilbo. We had to be set up by nine in the morning and would not leave until after six that evening. Bilbo had virtually no rest during the day, as there were thousands of people filing past. He behaved impeccably, bless him, returning the love showered upon him by so many.

Bilbo and I had visited Gerrans Primary School on the beautiful Roseland Peninsula early on in our career to give a talk to the children about beach safety, and in 2011 we returned by popular demand. Bilbo loved that particular journey as it involved crossing the River Fal at Carrick Roads Reach on the world-famous 'King Harry Ferry', a long-established ferry crossing going back, some said, five hundred years. Originally a manually propelled barge, it was replaced in 1888 by a submerged chain ferry bridge, using a steam engine to pull the ferry along the chains. I say 'world-famous' because it is officially billed as one of the top ten scenic ferry journeys of the world. It is truly breathtaking and the *clank, clank, clank* of the chain adds a certain atmosphere all of its own.

Bilbo would already be very excited before we arrived anywhere, sensing the slowing down of the car and, especially, the clicking of the indicator which meant that the window would come down in a moment and he could have a good look round. He seldom barked for attention, but then why would he need to? Just the sight of his big brown head would soon bring people flocking to him, asking questions or requesting a photograph. Bilbo would, of course, love every minute of the attention. At the ferry terminal we often had to queue, and as the crossing was made every ten minutes from alternate sides there was limited time for people to say hello to Bilbo. We usually caused chaos, as the timetable was quite tight! When, eventually, we drove onto the ferry, Bilbo watched everything with great interest. And as we began the crossing, the gentle motion and the slightly eerie clanking of the chain made him screw his head from side to side, intrigued.

While I was running errands in surrounding towns and villages like St Ives, Bilbo would hang his head out of the window as we inched our way through the narrow streets crawling with tourists. We would soon have children running alongside, chanting his name: 'Bilbo, Bilbo!' There were times when the traffic slowed down so much that people would start to take photos of him, which held the traffic up even more! It was the same almost everywhere he went. People always smiled when they saw him. Often when we were driving slowly in the summer traffic, I would open the window and he would stick his head out. Suddenly people's demeanour changed, and instead of wearing a grumpy, bored look, their faces would light up and many would be pointing and smiling at him. Bilbo exuded a charisma that could melt the worst of moods!

At one point it seemed as if he was featuring on local television almost daily. He was asked to lead the Truro City Carnival and was mobbed there too! He was even asked if he would open a new branch of a well-known supermarket in mid-Cornwall, he was such a popular celebrity.

On the one hand, we were busier than ever, chatting to everyone left, right and centre. But when it came to our local community, I went out of my way to avoid people. I didn't go to the beach at all. I didn't go to the pub for months either. It was all too painful. Now that I was no longer a lifeguard I felt awkward around people and became a bit of a recluse, to be honest. I stayed out of the way as much as possible, preferring to spend my time with Bilbo. One of our favourite walks was still the route around Chapel Carn Brea. Bilbo and I would go up there to avoid bumping into people and we'd walk around the hill and suddenly things didn't seem to be quite so bad. We had each other and he knew it by now. Bilbo saved me.

Mark still looked after Bilbo for me, and in reality the three of us would always be The Team. In a way Mark was his second owner. He always said that Bilbo had taken us both on so many random adventures, whether it was training him to do rescues for the television cameras, or appearing at dog events like the jamboree. Neither of us had been to a dog show in our lives before I got Bilbo, and I don't think we ever would have done if Bilbo hadn't come along.

The shift in our lifestyle undoubtedly affected Bilbo too. My daughter Alice noticed the change in him after we left the beach. She said that when Bilbo was younger and the times were good he was more playful and carefree but when we went through that bad time she thought Bilbo became more concerned about me – 'almost jealous' was how she put it. When we visited her house after she had Ruby, her first daughter, she reckoned Bilbo would get annoyed. And it's true that he would hang out for about half an hour and then he'd stand up and go and sit by the front door and let out this enormous sigh, as if to say: 'Can we go now?' He was always one to make his feelings very well known!

A German television company came to make a programme about our area of Cornwall and featured Bilbo and me. They showed Bilbo doing his work in schools, and me making my jewellery at my bench at Chez Noir and giving Bilbo a blow-dry with the industrial drier. But there was a poignant moment in the film when they took us down to the beach at Sennen. We couldn't go onto the sand, of course, as it was the summer and dogs weren't allowed. So they showed the two of us standing in the car park, looking down at the holidaymakers frolicking in the surf. We then turn sadly away and I say to Bilbo: 'Come on, boy, we can't go there today.'

Of course Bilbo missed the beach in the summertime because it was cool up by the lifeguard hut, whereas he found it much trickier to get cool inland. That's when having the use of his own VIP lake came in handy. He loved swimming up there and it suited me too because it was completely private and, again, I didn't have to see anybody.

Given that I was going through what, even for me, was a particularly solitary phase, I was at first reluctant to join some old colleagues from the early days of lifeguarding on a trip to visit a sick friend in Luxembourg. I'd met Mike Cattran in about 1978 when I moved to Gwynver beach after Sennen. He was the first lifeguard on Gwynver and he was appointed because of a drowning there in 1974. A fisherman had seen a couple setting off from Sennen harbour in a rowing boat and although he'd tried to tell them about the sea that day they didn't heed his warnings and the girl drowned when the boat capsized.

Mike and I became good friends and worked together on Gwynver until the mid-eighties when I left to go fishing. But we'd stayed in touch, on and off; he moved to Luxembourg and subsequently developed lung cancer. He was planning to come back and see everyone, but in 2012 he got worse and worse and it was obvious that he wasn't going to make it back. So a group of his friends who used to hang out together in the seventies rang me up and said, 'We're going over and we want you to come as well.'

Given the way I was feeling, which was glum to say the least, I was inclined not to bother. But as I thought about the old days, I remembered that Mike and I had a really good time down there. We got a lot of respect for the work we did because it was a dangerous beach. It still is. So I went to see him and I was glad that I did because he died not long afterwards, in October 2012. He was only fifty-nine.

We had a big send-off for him down on the beach at Sennen. He had left very specific instructions regarding his remains. He didn't want his ashes to be scattered anywhere; he wanted them to go in the sea and he wanted me to do it. That presented a tricky dilemma: how were we going to get his ashes *into* the sea as opposed to scattering them to the wind? The only way I could think of was by going out on a surfboard, diving in with the urn and taking it down to the bottom but if there were big waves on the chosen day, that could prove really difficult.

Mike's nickname was Fish, and on the day of the ceremony his ex-girlfriend turned up with a huge hollow ceramic fish. It was shaped like a carp but resembled a rugby ball. I thought: Brilliant, we'll stuff his ashes in there and go out to the point. As the waves come in I'll launch it into the face of the swell and it'll just go in and sink. So we did that. There are some amazing pictures of that day because there were a couple of holes in the fish, which I'd taped up, but before I threw it into the sea I took the tape off. And as it twisted through the air like a rugby ball, there was a spiral of ash that went down into the waves. Everybody was really moved by the whole thing.

Being with those guys, and having to say goodbye to one of us, really hammered it home to me: those carefree days of the seventies and eighties were long gone. In fact, such was my mood at the time, I felt as if *all* the good times were in the past. It was hard to feel optimistic about the future when it seemed to be nothing but one upsetting thing after another. Little did I know that it was about to get worse rather than better.

21

Moving On

I really loved living at Chez Noir. It was hardly palatial but it was just perfect for Bilbo and me. We could throw open our door in the morning and be presented with the most spectacular view a man – or dog – could wish for. OK, so it didn't have central heating, but Bilbo kept me warm in the winter. It was our own little kingdom up there.

I had a great relationship with the people who owned it too and felt like part of the family. So it was an almighty body blow when I had to leave at the beginning of 2013. I had known, however, that there had been long-term plans, and that they had been thinking of developing the shed for a while. I was devastated though, as the prospects of finding similar accommodation seemed remote, to say the least.

Some said: 'Well it's all right, Steve, you can go and sign on and they'll pay your rent wherever you go. You can get yourself a cottage in Penzance or something.' I was looking at them and thinking: What are you talking about? A cottage in Penzance! Why would I want to do that? Also, a lot of places don't take dogs, so what was I supposed to do with Bilbo?

I was at my wits' end and didn't know what to do. If I had been in the city, Bilbo and I could have ended up being on the street. That's how easily it could happen – I can see that now. It is just so easy for someone to fall on the wrong side and before you know it, you're homeless.

I had a job lined up on the Burghley Estate in Lincoln-shire for Bilbo and me, which would give us a roof over our heads for six weeks – albeit only a canvas one. Burghley House is home to the famous horse trials and is also the setting for the biggest obstacle course in the UK, called the Rat Race. It's a twenty-mile course and around sixty thousand people take part. Bilbo and I would be providing on-site security, as well as helping to construct the course itself. But the job wasn't starting until April so we were virtually homeless for about a month.

I had a friend, Linda, who I'd known back in the day but hadn't seen for over thirty years. Her husband, Hugh Stoneman, was a renowned master printer who worked with people like Sir Terry Frost RA and Grayson Perry – all the top artists you can think of. He did prints for all of them and he had a massive studio here in Penzance, the Stoneman Gallery. Sadly, he passed away in 2005 from cancer. Anyway, about the same time as I was being evicted from Chez Noir, I bumped into her in town and we got talking. I was trying to figure out what to do with my jew-ellery because I had made a few things but I needed to get them into the public arena in order to sell them. 'Why don't you put them into our gallery?' she offered.

I was so grateful for that lifeline. She took my jewellery and put it in the gallery and then she said that I could store my belongings in one of her outhouses. I couldn't thank her enough because without her I wouldn't have known what to do with it all! Although I lived in that shed as frugally as I could, when I came to move out the amount of junk I'd accumulated was unbelievable.

We may not have been a high-profile presence on the beach now, but Bilbo was still much in demand on the celebrity pooch circuit. The land that butts onto the ferry terminal on the Feock side of the River Fal is part of the Trelissick Estate, under the ownership of the National Trust since 1955, and is renowned for its variety of camellias, rhododendrons and azaleas. At one time it was owned by Sir Humphrey Gilbert, an explorer who had connections with – would you believe it – Newfoundland. So I thought it only fitting to accept and attend the National Trust's invitation to its open day and dog show one year. Not only were we invited to give a talk on Bilbo and the Newfoundland dog in general, but I would be allowed to set up Bilbo's stall and sell his merchandise. Even better, it adjoined a shady area where visitors could come and meet him and have the prerequisite photograph taken. We were very popular and were invited back for another year. Events like that were usually busy times for us as Bilbo's appearance would be advertised weeks in advance. Even the car-parking attendants would be keeping an eye out for his arrival, and always looked after us impeccably.

Because we lived at Land's End, most events would involve quite a drive for us and I adapted the back of our 4x4 to accommodate Billy. I collapsed the back seats so that it was big and roomy enough for him to fully stretch out on his travel bed. That way he could usually arrive relaxed and would only require a quick groom before going to work.

However it was quite often *me* who needed to lie down at the end of some events, as the queue to meet Bilbo could be relentless. He was so strong and I had to be constantly on my toes, as I was often amazed at people's lack of awareness regarding animal behaviour. They would let their own dogs freely wander all around Bilbo, who was of course attached to me. It was like having a two- to three-hour workout! One of the times we were at Trelissick he made a dash for a long-haired retriever and actually snapped his leash, which was hitched to the tow bar of the car at the time! They were good days, however, despite the difficulties I was having, and we met lots of interesting people along the way.

I was telephoned one day out of the blue and asked if Bilbo would appear on *Live With Gaby* on Channel 5 Breakfast because they had an empty slot. Of course I was more than happy to say yes and we travelled up to London later that week. Our chain hotel wasn't quite the Cannizaro but it would do.

The morning of the show, Bilbo – like many showbiz divas – was playing up because it was really hot in the hotel room. So I put him out in the car while I finished getting ready. I then locked the door of the hotel room and went out to the car, only to find Bilbo mucking around in there too. 'Bilbo, will you stop messing about!' I said in exasperation. 'We haven't got time for this. We're due on the telly!' Bilbo just gave me a look that said he wasn't about to do as he was told and I started to get a bit flustered because the taxi was due and I realized I had to go back into the hotel to get something. I shut the car door. 'Oh, please, no!' As soon as I closed it I realized that the car keys were inside!

Panicking, I phoned the studio. 'Er, there's a bit of a problem,' I said sheepishly to the worried-sounding producer. 'I'm afraid I've locked the guest of honour in the car!'

It took about three-quarters of an hour to free him. The AA man came and had to force the door open with wedges until he could open the catch. We made it to the studio on time, by the skin of our teeth, and the first thing the presenter Gaby Roslin said as we sat down was, 'Well, we're lucky to have you here, aren't we!' They certainly were. Not that Bilbo was fazed by all the panicking.

What is it they say, about never working with children and animals?

Nonetheless, the invitations continued to land on our mat, requesting the pleasure of Bilbo's company at such-and-such fundraising event or show, with me as his 'plus one'. In March 2013, shortly before we headed up to Lincolnshire for the Rat Race, he was even invited to a VIP dinner being held in honour of Susan Rescorla, the widow of 9/11 hero Rick.

Rick Rescorla, who was born in Cornwall but spent a good part of his life abroad, worked as head of security for Morgan Stanley in the Twin Towers in New York. He had foreseen the likelihood of a terrorist attack on the buildings and had implemented evacuation drills that were credited with saving many lives when al-Qaeda infamously struck on 11 September 2001. Singing some of his favourite Cornish songs through a loudhailer, he guided more than two thousand of his fellow workers in the South Tower to safety. His calm manner prevented panic and an even greater loss of life but sadly he died in the aftermath of the attack after going back inside the tower to look for stragglers.

Susan was visiting Cornwall for the unveiling of a monument in memory of her husband in Hayle, where he was born. Afterwards a dinner was held in Rick's honour and Bilbo and I were invited, along with other local 'celebrities'. It took place at the Porthminster Hotel in St Ives, which is a very upmarket hotel, and they didn't allow animals in there – especially great big hairy dogs. I'd left Bilbo in the car while we ate but when Susan found out she said, 'No, no, Bilbo has to come in!'

The hotel wouldn't go so far as to let him eat off a plate in the restaurant, but they did serve him up a platter in the foyer. He had an entire roast dinner: roast beef and vegetables, the same as everyone else. Like I say, people made exceptions for Bilbo all the time.

After the fine dining, it was back to earth with a bump when we tipped up at Burghley and discovered we had to make camp in the woods. At night Bilbo and I were the security in the compound and the woods. We would look after all the heavy plant that was kept there and the generators. We were working all the time. We'd sleep, obviously, but I had to get up at 3 a.m. to have a look around and then go back to bed again. As soon as I was awake Bilbo was ready. He was always on the case, Bilbo. He was with me one hundred per cent, that dog – really he was.

My friend Leroy came with us. It was our job to put up the inflatable obstacles on the enormous man-made lake. Enquiring where it was, I was told: 'White Water Lake is just beyond those trees over there.' Hmm, I thought. I wonder why it's called White Water Lake? When I eventually managed to see it, however, I instantly knew how it had got its name. It was an almost rectangular shape, with a solid bottom covered with – in some places – two metres or more of silt. At its deepest point it was about four metres. Trees and shrubs lined the two longest banks and a slight breeze blew through the length of the lake. Ah ha! I thought. So white water equals wind.

The inflatables arrived at the site pretty late but, even so, we figured we had plenty of time to get them erected. We were blessed with fabulous calm weather and Bilbo absolutely loved it because as we were so preoccupied he spent all day either swimming in the lake, looking at the wildfowl, or sunning himself on the bank. My and Leroy's problem, meanwhile, was that some of the inflatables were over four metres high, not exactly the easiest things to anchor, *and* there were six of them! We decided that they couldn't be anchored to the lake floor as it would damage the lining, so we would have to rely on weight alone to keep them in place.

Leroy and I had been at it all day since breakfast and still hadn't managed to get everything secured. The workload was increasing for us and – to add insult to injury – everyone seemed to have forgotten about us that day and hadn't sent us any lunch. By seven o'clock in the evening, Lee was getting really grumpy through lack of food. He got so angry he ended up throwing a whole lot of rope at me in the boat. 'I've had enough!' he shouted, as all this rope landed on top of me.

OK, let's not push it anymore, I thought. I knew I couldn't complete the job on my own – I had to have his

help. 'Let's just finish these ones off and we'll call it a day,'
I suggested amiably. So we finished and walked back to the
camp but Leroy was still really angry because not only had
he not had any food, no one was coming to take him back
to his digs either. I was the only one who lived in the forest,
there were no facilities for anybody else and we didn't
really have any food there either. He was so angry he
jumped on the back of a motorbike that was lying around,
fired it up, and drove off in a right temper.

I suppose the bike sounded not dissimilar to the quad
at Sennen, which Bilbo associated with going for a ride on
the beach. It was a sound he'd grown to love and whenever
he heard it he'd get up and go and find the quad. Anyway,
Lee drove off and went a good three-quarters of a mile to
what was called the 'construction site', intent on having
a burn-up to get rid of his aggression. He hammered up
there, stopped and turned round to admire the view and
was astounded to see dear Bilbo, tongue hanging out, lol-
loping up behind him! And he was ten years old at the time
– a veritable pensioner in dog years!

Seeing Bilbo immediately changed Leroy's mood of
course, and he ended up walking the motorbike back with
Bilbo at his side with a big smile on his face – although he
was still hungry!

We worked hard at Burghley but I was still feeling anxious about where Bilbo and I were going to live once it was
over. People kept saying to me, 'You'll have to sign on and
get your rent paid.' But I'd say, 'What are you talking about?
I'm not going to sign on. I'll manage myself.' All the same,
I didn't know exactly *how* I was going to do that.

Luckily, a place became vacant at about the same time.

It was an old railway carriage perched on top of the cliff, not far from Chez Noir. My neighbour Ian owned it and in the past it had been let to holidaymakers. I went to see him and to my surprise he said, 'Well, there's no one in there at the moment, you can move in whenever you like.' I came back in the middle of May with Bilbo and we moved in. It was fantastic compared to Chez Noir, which was pretty ramshackle. It had originally been brought across the fields by tractor in the 1930s because they couldn't get it up the lane. It was much smaller even than Chez Noir – if that were possible – but draught free and so much warmer. I considered myself really, really lucky to find it.

The owner had put cladding on the side and a new roof on and bay windows in to accommodate a sink, as it didn't have one. Through the window you could see the sea and Cape Cornwall, and the coastal path lay just beyond the bamboo gate. There was a lovely secluded garden too, which was sheltered from the wind by a variety of hedges. Bilbo and I settled in quite happily, I have to say. I called it – what else – Chez Choo Choo.

22

Poorly Pet

The philosophy I have come to adopt in life is that basically you get what you ask for. That proved to be true when
Bilbo and I returned to Burghley the following year. I was
not looking forward to the journey: 350 miles, which would
take at least six hours to drive. I'd been thinking for days:
This is going to be an awful journey; it's going to be terrible. It proved even worse than I'd been expecting – to the
extent that I even got pulled by the police for being all over
the road. I was completely lost and was so busy looking at
the map.

Anyway, we finally made it and we actually had a good
time working there, although it was hard graft as usual.
Bilbo even had a holiday romance! He chummed up with a
border collie called Nancy, who belonged to one of the
guys who was working there. She and Bilbo used to go
swimming in the lake every day. Every morning they'd trot
off together and have a brilliant time. He had a great
summer of freedom swimming in the lake with his friend.
It was wonderful to see him so happy.

After six weeks of working we were really tired and all

I wanted to do was get home. However, I was dreading the journey again, to an almost obsessive degree. The last two days it was only Bilbo and myself left on site. The campsite had been pulled down and the Portakabin office I'd been staying in had gone so I was sleeping in an articulated lorry for those two nights as it had a berth in the back. Bilbo had to sleep in my car because the lorry was too high for him to climb into.

There was just this lorry, a digger and a dumper truck left and it was my last job to wait for the drivers to turn up and collect them the following day, which was a Thursday. Then Bilbo and I could head home to Cornwall. I was up at first light the next morning because I'd been used to getting up at half five to prepare breakfast for the workers. The guy was due to come with a low loader for the big swing shovel and the dumper at about seven, so I jumped down from the cab, slammed the door, and took Bilbo for his morning constitutional.

But when we came back from our walk and I tried to open the door, the lorry had automatically locked itself. Worse, my wallet, phone and the keys to the excavator that the guy was going to come and pick up in a minute were in there too. All the windows were firmly shut and I couldn't break into it because it was a brand new lorry and had double security on everything. I started to panic, thinking that I must have dropped the keys while we were walking. So I went back around the track with Bilbo but couldn't find them. And that was the start of our journey home. From there it just went like a block of dominoes and got worse and worse, to the point where I was laughing in the end because it was so flipping unbelievable.

I realized that this sort of thing must happen all the time on construction sites, and that the guy who was coming to pick up the excavator must have a spare set of keys, which of course he did. So we loaded it up and he said, 'When you get into the lorry just put the keys in an envelope and send them back to the hire company.' Then, just as he was going, he said, 'What are you going to do? Have you got a phone?' and I said, 'No, it's all in the cab.' Fortunately he had the number of the construction company on his phone and he rang the boss and told him to make sure the guys brought a spare set of keys to the lorry when they came up that afternoon.

They were coming from Amersham, which was a two-hour drive up the M1, so I sat in the car with Bilbo, killing time. Luckily all our stuff was in the car because it was packed up ready to come home, so Bilbo's food and water were in there. But I didn't have anything to eat, which was fair enough as it was my fault. Meanwhile, I tried to start my car and, of course, it wouldn't start. So I'm now sat in the middle of this field with no phone, no food, only Bilbo's water to drink, and a flat battery. There was nothing for it but to wait for these guys to turn up at two o'clock.

Finally, they turned up and I said, 'Great, where are the keys?' They looked at me blankly: 'What keys?' So they had to drive all the way back again to get them! But they did at least phone the AA for me before they left.

Eventually the guy from the AA turned up and announced that he couldn't fix it and would have to take it to Mercedes in Peterborough. I said, 'No way is it going to Mercedes anywhere – it's going back to Penzance.' It was a friend's car and I had only borrowed it because mine had blown up the day before I was due to leave (it was an ill-fated trip on the travel front!). But then he looked at my policy and said I was entitled to a replacement car. 'I'll get somebody to come and pick your car up and then we'll go to Peterborough and get you a hire car and you can go on your way,' he said. Great, I thought. We'll soon be home.

But as it was, I spent all day waiting in this field for the guys to come back and I had to sleep there that night too, in the Mercedes with Bilbo. There wasn't a lot of room, I can tell you! Fortunately there were some workmen who were staying on for a few extra days' work. They got to hear that I was stranded and they brought me a Chinese take-away that evening. No spoon or anything though, so I was eating it like a dog! Bilbo had some crispy seaweed. It was a grim night. It was so uncomfortable trying to sleep in the car with Bilbo and all our stuff that at four o'clock in the morning I got out and went and lay under the lorry and slept there.

The AA came and picked up the Mercedes the next morning and we were taken to Peterborough with the car on the back. The AA man liked Bilbo but even so he wouldn't let him ride with us in the cab so he had to stay in the Mercedes on the back of the lorry. Goodness knows what he made of being so high up. When we arrived at the car hire place they pointed to a minuscule hatchback and said, 'That's the car you get as a replacement.' And I said: 'But what are we going to do with Bilbo?' As there was no way he was going to fit in there with all our gear.

The rental people loved Bilbo too, so they set about trying to find us something more suitable to his size. It ended up costing me a hundred odd quid, mind you, but they upgraded us to a Volkswagen Passat, which was brand new and plenty big enough for Bilbo. It had sat nav and everything and I thought: This is brilliant! I didn't mind paying the money – I was so fed up by this time I just wanted to get home. I was tired after six weeks of working eighteen-hour days and getting up twice in the night to do security checks.

So we headed off and the plan was to drive as far as Poole, where my cousin lives, and stop the night there. We'd drive on to Sennen the next day. To cut a long story short, I got to Poole, parked up in her driveway and hung my keys up in her conservatory. But of course she got broken into in the night, didn't she! The burglars stole the keys to my hire car, tried to drive it away but couldn't start it because it was such a new car, and must have thrown the keys away in frustration because they were nowhere to be found.

I rang the police and they came and fingerprinted it but they couldn't get me a replacement car because it was a Bank Holiday and the Devon Show and there wasn't a hire car to be had for love nor money. So I didn't get out of there until the Monday or Tuesday – it was days anyway. And when I told my daughter Alice the story she said, 'Dad, do you know what? That all started with one bad thought.' I said, 'Come on, Alice, no it didn't.' But then of course when I sat and thought about it, it probably did. I asked for it because I'd kept going on about how bad the journey was going to be – and it was.

That summer of 2014 was very hot in Cornwall and it was very, very warm in the evenings. There was a night in July when I got a thermometer out in the bathroom, where

Bilbo slept in the summertime, and it registered 26°C. Bilbo had been drinking loads of water all day and I couldn't seem to cool him down. It must have been uncomfortable for him, having such a heavy coat.

Ordinarily he slept very well – I never had a problem with him during the night (the incident involving the Bilbo-sized hole in my door at Chez Noir notwithstanding!) because he always had plenty of fresh air and exercise. I wouldn't usually hear a peep out of him until he woke me up at six thirty. I wasn't expecting him to wake up on this particular night, because he never did, so I wasn't listening out for him. But when I checked on him the next morning the poor lad had been sick in the wet room.

It was a Sunday and I rang our local vet's, the Rosevean Veterinary Practice in Penzance, and explained what had happened, just to check in with them really. I guess I was looking for reassurance. But to my surprise they told me to bring him in immediately. When I got Bilbo to their surgery the vet took Bilbo in for tests. 'I'm afraid Bilbo is very poorly, Steve,' the vet said. 'Because he was sick in his sleep, he has inhaled his vomit which has given him aspiration pneumonia.' He explained that it occurs when food or fluid gets into the lungs and was extremely serious because it had affected his kidneys and liver, which were both now failing. 'You might have to think about euthanasia if he's not right by tomorrow afternoon,' he added, with a worried look on his face.

I couldn't believe my ears. There was no way my strong healthy boy could be that ill! The vet was surely being too pessimistic. I said, 'Now, just you hold on a minute, Chief. I don't believe that for one minute. There's something

wrong with him; you're the vet – you fix what's wrong with
him and he'll come out of here.' I believed it one hundred
per cent – I had to – because there was no way I was ready
to say goodbye to Bilbo. I knew it was up to me to keep the
pressure on the vets until they made him well so I said,
'Listen, he's insured to the hilt, that dog. I want you to find
out what's wrong with him. End of. Do whatever it takes.'

So he had an ECG (an electrocardiogram to assess the
electrical and muscular functions of his heart), blood tests
– the works. And they couldn't find anything wrong with
him. His bloods showed nothing wrong at all. The only
thing they came up with was that his heart was slightly
enlarged and was beating faster than normal.

I was also encouraged by the vet saying what great
shape Bilbo was in for an eleven-year-old dog. They said
he was more like a seven-year-old in terms of his health
and general well-being.

I kept the fact that Bilbo was at the vet's quiet at first
because I didn't want anybody to know. I didn't want
anyone believing that he was ill – I wanted them to think
he was well. The way I see it, if you're constantly thinking
about something – or someone – being unwell, you're
asking for them to be unwell. Whereas, if you keep thinking
of them as being happy and running around, that's the vibe
you're putting out. I believe everything is connected by
energy.

I knew Mark would want to see Bilbo, just in case, so I
rang him and asked him to come and visit Bilbo at the vet's.
I said, 'He needs you.' Because we were a team and we dealt
with everything together. With lifeguarding you make the
best friends of your life because you see them every day.

You spend sixty hours a week together, either on the beach or hanging out after work. When Mark arrived I sat him in my car and told him what had gone on. I said, 'The Team needs to be back together, the three of us.'

We went into the clinic to see him. Mark was expecting Bilbo to look quite ill after everything I'd just told him, but was happy to see that he just looked the same as he always did. He looked fit, and it was nearly August so he was just breaking out of ginger into sun-bleached blond. He said to me, 'He doesn't look bad at all, J'mo.'

I gave Bilbo to Mark and we took him outside for a wee. He was having trouble with his waterworks because every-thing had been affected by the pneumonia. He hadn't had a wee since he'd arrived at the vet's and they were worried about him not passing water, but he went straight away with Mark.

I would go and sit with Bilbo every day from about eleven in the morning until the surgery shut at seven o'clock – just as I had with my mum. It was fine weather so I'd take him outside and we'd sit under a tree. I would take his brushes and groom him and talk to him all the time. I think that attention, me sitting with him every day, made all the difference. He had so much love poured over him, plus great treatment from the vets and nurses. He was having electrolytes to keep him hydrated, and one of the vets, Anita, told me early on that she was going to put 'something extra' in. She gave him glucose, and that's what made him rally.

As I sat with Bilbo under the tree, remembering all the happy times we'd had together, I thought about producing a book that would be educational for children. I wanted to teach them about the things that, in my experience, most problems arose from. Things like not spotting a rip, digging in sand, swimming where there's floating ropes, jumping off harbour walls, tomb-stoning – all that sort of stuff. The booklet I'd written about Bilbo was really just a little story about him. There were flags in it, but it wasn't written specifically with education in mind. It was really just a memento of Bilbo for children to take home with them after their holiday – that's all it was.

But the one I now wanted to do was different, and while I was sitting under the tree with him I started plotting it out. Over the coming days I managed to write it all down, with drawings of flags and illustrations of tides. I guess it helped take my mind off worrying about Bilbo a bit too.

A friend came down one afternoon to see us and brought me an ice cream. Bilbo was just sitting there attached to his drip and I could tell by her face that she thought he looked really awful that day. He hadn't shown any interest in his food for days, but he saw the ice cream and started dribbling out of the corner of his mouth. It was brilliant, because that was the moment we both realized he was going to make it. Of course we gave him some. Bilbo loved ice cream and vanilla was his absolute favourite flavour.

I never doubted that he would get better – although there were eleven vets at that practice and not one of them thought he would make it out of there alive.

He improved quite quickly once they started his medication and he came home on the Friday evening, having been in there for almost a week. Talking to my friend about what a scare he'd given us, she remembered that he'd been acting strangely a couple of days before he got sick. I was working at her house in Penzance and he disappeared. She said she couldn't find him anywhere and started to think: The monkey's gone up to the road.

But when she went into the field, there he was, lying under a tree. She said she thought: How strange, he's never done that before. It was the Friday before I had to take him to the vet. 'He was really weird,' she said. 'I had to coax him to come with me as he looked as though he wanted to be on his own and for me to clear off.'

It all started to make sense now: they say that poorly animals often take themselves off to be alone when they are ill. Poor Bilbo, he had had a close call for sure, and I for one never wanted to go through that again.

23

Heartbreak

Bilbo was discharged with a month's supply of heart medication, which the vet said he would have to be on for the rest of his life. I gave thanks again for having such a good insurance policy! However, one of the side effects of the heart tablets was that they made him sick and for the next three months I was up with him every night. Every two hours I would hear him being sick, get up and clear it all away and clean him up. It sounds upsetting, but he never seemed distressed. Embarrassed perhaps, because he would look at me as if to say, 'Sorry, boss.'

Had I observed him in distress, however, that would have been different. I would have had to consider his quality of life and whether I should be thinking about having him put to sleep, but he was still wagging his tail and making that face of his – when he scrunched up his lips and looked like he was smiling. He ate his food and was happy. We never missed one morning's walk, whatever the weather. He wasn't incontinent and his limbs were in fairly good shape so he was always able to cock his leg.

He was all right when his medication wasn't making

him sick, and when he was ill it was always at night when he lay down. I talked to Paul, the vet, about it and he said, 'You might have to think about his diet because you're feeding him dried food, aren't you?' I was, and up to that point I hadn't been wetting it for him. So what was happening was that he was eating because he was hungry, it would then swell up inside him, and because his heart was enlarged it would press on everything and he'd be sick. So I started wetting the dried kibble and waiting until it was already expanded before he ate it, and that helped a bit.

Even so, the vomiting went on until my friend Linda offered to cook specially for Bilbo. She has dogs of her own, a dachshund Jack Russell cross called Toulouse and a Norfolk terrier called Weetie, and she fell in love with Bilbo. I find it only fair to say at this point that had it not been for Linda, I do not know how I would have coped with Bilbo alone. I was trying to pull myself from the depths of despair as it was and she was a pillar of strength. The attention and love she showed towards Bilbo was true and unconditional. She mixed boiled white rice with cooked chicken and liquidized it until it was like porridge. Bilbo loved it and got really well on that. I used to hand-feed him with a wooden spoon. That's part of the reason he survived – because a lot of effort was put into getting him well. She used to make him liver jerky bites as well. I was broke and she was buying a lot of his food. It was a very costly business and although I could not contribute at that point, I knew that in time I would repay her.

As well as her gallery, Linda had a couple of holiday lets and about six acres at Orchard Flower Farm, her home just outside Penzance. It's completely unique and Bilbo and I spent a lot of time there. Bilbo liked it a lot. He got on well with her dogs – and five cats!

And despite his illness, he was still the old Bilbo. On my birthday that October I received a remote-controlled 'Chinook' helicopter. Although essentially a toy, it required concentration, time and patience just to get the hang of it. Billy and I had been invited to a friend's house for supper and afterwards I was demonstrating my new toy in the middle of quite a spacious room.

Out of the corner of my eye I noticed Bilbo becoming annoyed, not just with the whine the toy was making, but also that I was occupying *my* – and everyone else's – time with something other than *him*. I could see him moving his head up and down to attract my attention. Well you can just wait, my lad, I thought, turning my attention back to the tiny helicopter.

I had already mastered the take-off and landing bit and was now trying to perfect the hover, a manoeuvre that required some considerable concentration. Well, Bilbo had had enough of being ignored and, stamping his feet, began his pathetic, 'Look at me! Look at me!' bark. No one paid him any attention, however, all being more intrigued whether I would crash the thing or not when, as quick as a flash, this suddenly agile, brown surface-to-air missile took it out with one sweetly combined leap and bite!

I could see him thinking, Hah, that's the end of that, as he spat the bits out and nonchalantly padded back to where his bed was, tail held high with that air of, 'Didn't hurt me' about him. Yeah, you can act all cool, my lad, I thought, smiling to myself, knowing that he must have been smarting from the rotor blades as they smacked into his chops.

Still, Bilbo 1–Helicopter 0.

I was desperate to find work because I needed to earn money. I'd spent all my savings because I didn't want to sign on or get involved in any of that government benefit stuff. I have in the past – there were times when I had to – but the grief that came with it was awful. My overheads weren't very big because my rent at Chez Choo Choo was reasonable, and I wasn't going out anywhere because looking after Bilbo was occupying all of my time.

But I couldn't get a proper job because it was taking me until half ten each day before I was ready to do anything. I would get up at first light, about half six, and give Bilbo his tablets, make sure he'd had everything he needed, and then take him for a walk, bring him back and groom him. So it was difficult to find regular work because most jobs involved starting at half eight. And in any case what employer would let a worker stop what they were doing to attend to their dog? If I ever had to go anywhere without him I would have to try and sneak off without him noticing, and what a manoeuvre that would be! I couldn't go fishing again – even if I'd wanted to, which I didn't – because that would have involved being at sea for eight days at a stretch and I couldn't leave Bilbo.

Once again my friend Linda came to my rescue. 'You know, Steve, I've got a lot of things that need doing around this place and really need somebody to work here,' she said to me one day. I started working there, tending the jungle – I mean garden! – at Orchard Flower Farm, a task akin to painting the Forth Bridge. By the time I'd managed to clear one area and moved on to the next, everything was beginning to grow back! But slowly, bit by bit, I started to get it under control, put in a vegetable patch and planted a small orchard.

I also got the job to redecorate her house inside and out, plus the gallery and the holiday let. She accepted that I could only work four hours a day because of my commitment to Bilbo, so the arrangement suited us both. It was also good for Bilbo, because he could come with me to work. He used to love lying in the pools in the stream that runs along the bottom of her garden. She said he was like a hippo, because you couldn't see him – there were just these eyes looking up. He'd be in there for ages, wallowing.

At lunchtime we'd sit at the large farmhouse table, which was just the right height for Bilbo to rest his head on! Before his latter days, when he could only eat chicken, he used to have minced beef and we took a great photo of him staring at this tub of minced beef on the kitchen table. He didn't make a move but he just stared fixedly at it!

As Bilbo became older I adapted our walks so that, when he was in his sunset years, it was an almost flat walk. I also began to feed him two smaller meals a day rather than the one big one. Scrambled egg was a favourite breakfast, mixed with his dried food. Then he would lie down and rest – you could not say sleep as he always had one eye open.

I was struggling at the time with my private life and was worrying as to how to pay the bills so I set up my workbench in Choo Choo and began to spend time building my jewellery stock up. Most days Bilbo was content just to sit outside, guarding the door, although sometimes he would scratch on the door or simply call out to be let in for some attention. Many an hour we spent sitting outside, watching the waves and simply enjoying each other's company. Some days however could be grim, when it was wet for weeks on end with thick mud everywhere. We had no means to dry towels or clothes but fortunately those times were few and far between.

Bilbo liked to have a vantage point at all times and in his very favourite spot he was even beginning to make a depression in the ground! Every morning he took up his 'on guard' position where he could keep an eye on every exit and entrance, yet close enough so he could let me know if I was running late for his morning walk, for example. If he thought I was taking too long, I would soon hear him scratching at the door and then running off in the direction of the gate, shaking his head from side to side, mouth wide open, looking back at me straight in the eye, saying, '*Come on, Captain.*'

On mornings when, due to foul weather or just apathy, I didn't want to do anything, Bilbo encouraged me not to give in. That 'Come on, Captain' look made me want to man up and get out there.

Afternoons also took on a new complexion for us with a daily afternoon walk. I always tried to vary the location, having learnt where some obscure walks were when we used to check the coastal emergency telephones. Bilbo remembered each route every time as if it was his 'patch'. Always being aware of potential back leg problems, I kept his afternoon walks deliberately short and as a change we would sometimes go up to 'his' lake and he would spend half an hour or more just swimming up and down.

The rest of the time he would just come along with me, doing whatever I was doing. Sometimes our late walk would take us past a pub and we would often stop for a beer and a chat. Bilbo was known locally as a celebrity and was always made welcome with fresh water being brought for him!

Most evenings, after his supper, Bilbo would again adopt his 'on guard' position under the bush by the kitchen door. He would have stayed there all night if he could but I had to bring him inside as Mr Fox would come by in the night to wind him up, and consequently everyone else in the vicinity!

On cold, draughty, stormy evenings, however, there was nothing better than Bilbo lying all over me, keeping me warm.

Even as an old dog he still liked the ladies and age never curtailed his romancing ways. When Andy, a pal of Linda's, visited one day, he left his collie in the car because she was on heat but as soon as he opened the door to leave, Bilbo shot past everybody and dived straight into the back seat. I'd never seen him move so fast! For a big dog he could certainly move. We still played hide and seek from time to time and he never forgot the special whistle I had for him. Shame he appeared to have developed selective hearing in his old age, though!

When we arrived home one winter's night, it was already dark and damp and I was struggling with both hands full, trying to unfasten our gate, when I inadvertently dropped his rope. It had only been a few seconds, but when I turned round, he had vanished! Grrr! I thought: There must be a bitch in season around here. I was furious as it was raining that sleety, horrible rain, and to cap it all I had a knee injury which was rather debilitating at the time. More worrying to me, however, was the fact that Bilbo's rope had a large knot at the end of it. I was concerned that it would become jammed somewhere, effectively trapping him. Even with his thick coat, I feared for him if he had to stay outside all night in his condition, and he would need his medication too. So I trudged off into the night, torch in hand, to search for him.

There were two possible farms I thought he could have headed to, but which one had he chosen? I looked along the track and eventually found a recent paw print pointing me in the right direction. There was no mistaking it – it was definitely his paw print. No other dog in the vicinity had feet anywhere near as big as his! Tracking him past the first farm, I doubled back and scoured around, then double-checked the shadows and waited. Nothing. The second possible destination was not far along the road and I soon picked up his trail again. However, it vanished somewhat short of the house. Once again I checked all around, then double-checked, and then I heard this doleful, whiny bark coming from what sounded like the field in front of the house. And there he was, looking very embarrassed, trapped by his rope on a granite stile, sitting, if you don't mind, in a puddle of slush! I don't know who was more relieved, him or me. We had both been out in the sleet and wind for over an hour. Grateful to be back inside our cosy carriage, I fed the pair of us and we eventually settled down for the night.

*

We continued visiting schools and Bilbo enjoyed it. He always knew when he was going to be meeting his public because I would give him an extended grooming session beforehand. It did start to take it out of him a bit in the last year, though, because I noticed he would be really tired the next day. But when he was working he never used to give up and sit down. He knew when his jacket was on that something was expected of him and he changed – into a well-behaved dog!

And his fan club was still going strong. Shortly before he became ill, a family came to see him with their little boy. They were from the Oxford area and they emailed me and said they were down and would it be all right if they met Bilbo. They came to the railway carriage and brought him a bag of dog treats. They spent the morning having photographs taken with him. It made the little lad's day, meeting Bilbo and receiving a certificate to say that he had.

I had to go into hospital to have an operation for a hernia. It had been going on for a long time and it was just getting worse and worse and so had to be sorted. Bilbo had gone to stay at Orchard Flower Farm with Toulouse and Weetie as he was used to spending a lot of time there. All the dogs had been bought matching stripy beds and Bilbo had been given a waterbed as a present. It had some kind of sponge in it that you filled with water and would stay at a constant temperature. When he lay on it, it would never get any hotter than his body temperature. It was brilliant in the summer especially, but he didn't always want to lie on it! He preferred to lie on the cool kitchen floor, where he often left a Bilbo-shaped imprint of dust!

We'd managed to get on top of the sickness now and

things were going all right, but then, in May 2015, things started to go a bit awry again. It was the weekend and Bilbo appeared rather listless. On the Sunday he was very slow on his morning walk and in fact we did not do the full circuit, which was most unusual. I took his temperature and as it was a bit high I phoned the vet, who advised bringing him in first thing Monday morning. They ran all the tests again and couldn't find anything wrong with his organs, but his heartbeat was beginning to speed up. They kept him in overnight and by the next morning his heart rate had gone up to 160, when it should have been no more than 80.

David, another of the vets, told me: 'Basically his heart is going out of control. We're going to try him on human beta-blockers, which will lower Bilbo's heart rate.' We waited to see how successful the drugs were, but they only managed to bring it down to 120. That, combined with having a temperature, must have been making him feel quite unwell and uncomfortable because he couldn't seem to settle. This was different from the first time he'd been ill. This time I knew there would be no happy ending. Soon I would be having that awful discussion with the vet again.

When I arrived at the vet's on the Wednesday morning, dear Bilbo raised his head in recognition but his tail was barely wagging. Suddenly he looked very frail to me and my heart sank. The nurse who had been with him all night said he'd had a 'reasonable' night but that he was obviously pleased to see me. It was late in May and the weather was warm. We agreed that outside in the garden would be the best place for him, in the shade. So, as Billy was a bit wobbly on his pins, we wrapped him in a blanket and carried him, still attached to his saline drip, stretcher-like, out into the leafy garden. Bilbo, thankful to be out in the fresh air, looked comfortable.

David was really good; he was very understanding because he knew that I was hurting. He said to me, 'You know, it is time to think about that decision, Steve.'

I said, 'I know, but he has only been on the antibiotics for one day. Let's see how he is tonight and I'll think about it tomorrow.'

But he said, ever so gently, 'I think you need to think about it *today*. Anyway,' he added, 'I have some stuff to do, so have a think and I will be back in a while.'

I knew he was right, but still I hesitated. After all, Bilbo had got well once before when they thought he wouldn't, hadn't he? Who was to say he wouldn't get well again? I was clutching at straws but in the end it was Bilbo himself who made the decision for me. We had been sitting there in the shade for about two or three hours. Just sitting, in a bubble, when suddenly he sat upright and made a whimpering noise. I tried to comfort him but he wasn't having any of it and shook me away! He stared at me for what seemed a long time, then slowly laid his head down on my lap. I lifted his head up and, looking into his beautiful amber eyes, I knew what he was telling me. 'I have been a loyal and true companion to you and we have had amazing times, but you must not let your tears get in the way of what you have to do for me today.'

At that point a nurse came to check his temperature and, as a routine, I checked his capillary refill. You do that by pressing gently on your pet's gums with your finger, which forces blood out of the small blood vessels, or capillaries. When you release the pressure the blood should return almost immediately to the vessels. However, with animals that are in – or going into – shock, it takes far longer. To my dismay, Bilbo's capillary refill rate was awful. We decided he might be better off on oxygen and hurriedly moved him indoors to the veterinary operating theatre. There was a lot of initial rushing around, but Bilbo was quickly put on oxygen, with a mask to help him breathe, and he soon settled down. Suddenly it was peaceful and quiet again.

David came in and sat on the floor beside us. 'How do you feel about it now?' he asked quietly. I could hardly speak and was trying to be brave and not lose it. Suddenly, Bilbo became agitated and started making a whimpering sound. 'I know, he told me himself,' I said sadly. 'I know what needs to be done now.'

Warmly laying his arm on my shoulder and rising, David said, 'Well done. It is the right thing. I will go and load three big ones up for him.'

There was silence in that operating theatre again, apart from the faint hiss of Bilbo's oxygen cylinder. So there we were, together; me stroking him and telling him what a good boy he was. My boy. I sat there in a daze and filled in the relevant forms, giving my permission for him to be put to sleep. The whole practice was brilliant that afternoon. They closed the operating theatre down and the nursing team and reception staff, always so helpful, were in tears.

David too, when he came back in, was crying. 'I don't normally get affected like this,' he said. I had been wondering whether he would sedate Bilbo first but David said, 'Look, he has a mainline straight into his back leg where the drip is already connected. That is why there are three of these.' He showed me three large syringes filled with a sinister blue liquid. 'This is why we call it putting to sleep,' he explained. 'The first one will put him into a coma, and the second two will stop his heart. You just keep talking to him and fussing him, and I will tap you on the shoulder when the first one has gone in. Are you ready?'

Looking at him, almost in disbelief, I tearfully nodded and turned back to Bilbo. 'I love you so much. You are a good boy,' I repeated over and over. Bilbo did not even flinch, he just went to sleep, and it could not have been more than ten seconds. It was very peaceful for him. Afterwards, I was left alone with him for an hour and, still talking to him, groomed him to perfection. He looked so beautiful, even in death.

I realized it was the only thing that could have happened that day; I knew it was. I'd kept him going for nearly a year and it had been a really good year too. If I had let the vet go ahead with what he wanted to do the year before, Bilbo and I would have missed out on all that time together. An extra year in a dog's life is like a person being given an extra decade.

All his brothers and sisters died at ten and his mother went at ten, but Bilbo was twelve when he died, which is a good age for a large dog like him. He had a fantastic innings for his breed. Big dogs don't often go past ten. Sometimes they don't even make eight. I took solace from that, and from knowing that he'd had a fantastic life.

But the prospect of going home to the noisy silence of my railway carriage without him was just awful. Leroy met me outside and came over and gave me a hug. There were tears in his eyes and although I felt wiped out I very much wanted to tell him what had happened at the end, and how I knew that it was time for Bilbo to say goodbye.

Leroy tried to get me to focus on all the people Bilbo had affected, and all the good things he'd done. He said, 'It wasn't just children who were affected by you and Bilbo, it was everyone. There are a lot of people out there – adults, kids, animals – who don't have what Bilbo had. He was worshipped. He was very privileged because he had the best of the best until the very end.'

About a week before Bilbo passed away Leroy had taken a really beautiful picture of me cuddling Bilbo outside my place. The sun was going down into the sea and we both looked so happy. As I looked at it I wondered: how was I going to go on without him?

One of the hardest things was having to break the news to Bilbo's fans, many of whom of course were children. I couldn't bear the thought of having to tell people, because then it would be real, but I realized I owed it to them to let them know – however painful it was for me – so I posted the sad news on his Facebook page.

'Just to let you know that my lovely, lovely Bilbo/best friend/saviour, slipped his moorings late this afternoon and has sailed off without me. RIP Bilbo, my Gwynver Supreme 2003–2015.'

24

Bilbo's Legacy

After Bilbo died I didn't want to see anybody. My life had revolved around Bilbo for ten years and now he was gone there didn't seem to be any point to anything. One of the small things I felt I could do after he died was to donate his special waterbed to the veterinary practice so that other poorly pets could benefit from it. I wrote them a letter as well, telling them how much their kindness had meant to me, and to Bilbo.

Other than that, I did nothing. I didn't go into town – I hardly went out at all. I couldn't bear the thought of having to communicate with people. When I did, the conversation was inevitably about Bilbo but would quickly turn into a story about their own pet's demise and I could not cope with any of that. Some even capped it off with a: 'Well, at the end of the day, he was only a dog.'

Other people – often complete strangers – were incredibly kind, though. Thousands and thousands shared the news on social media that Bilbo had passed away and I received some lovely messages of condolence from all around the world. His obituary went viral and was even in the national press.

An artist from North London sent me a beautiful crayon drawing of Bilbo. She'd never met him but she read about him dying and drew a picture from a photograph. It's about forty centimetres square and showed him on the beach at Sennen in his prime, while he was working. She said in her letter that it had taken her twenty-two hours to do. She had it framed and delivered by couriers. It means a lot to me, that picture, and I cherish it. It hangs on the wall in Chez Choo Choo, above the spot where he used to sleep, and I look at it every day.

Friends tried to cheer me up. Lloyd said to me, 'You gave that dog the best life that any dog could ever have.' And I know I did. I also knew that Bilbo had left a very big hole in all of our lives, not just mine. Mark and Leroy too – they both wept buckets when he left us. I gained a great deal of comfort from talking to those friends who had known him best. We did a lot of reminiscing in the weeks and months after he died. Mark always used to say that Bilbo had stayed in puppy mode his whole life. Not in terms of his behaviour, but in his personality. He was always a laugh and even when he was young we used to say, 'He's going to go on for a while, this one.'

We'd always tried our best to keep him healthy so that he would live a long life. 'Do you remember being at that dog show with Bilbo, when the woman was feeding her dog pork pies?' Mark reminded me. 'That massive black and white Newfoundland – the Landseer? It was fluffy and big like Bilbo but when you put it next to Bilbo you couldn't even tell they were the same breed! Do you remember we looked at it and thought, "Poor thing", because it was knackered, even from just waddling along, and there she was feeding it fat-laden pork pies!'

Bilbo enjoyed the best life possible and gave so much in return. Yes, I did grieve for him, but I also rejoice in his life and all the happiness he brought me and so many others – both young and old. I feel so privileged that he chose me as the companion he wanted to spend the rest of his life with. He was a complete 'one-off', was Billy. Totally unique.

I had not been sleeping too well during Bilbo's last months because he had been up a lot in the night again, being sick. After he died I started to drink too much, and you don't sleep very well when you're drinking a lot. I have always been someone who could fall asleep at a moment's notice. I would put my head down and after five minutes I'd be asleep. If I woke up – for instance when Bilbo was poorly – I would be able to go right back to sleep again afterwards. But that had all changed. Now I would lie awake for hours, grieving. Alcohol helped to dull the pain up to a point and I was certainly drinking a lot. Things came to a head a couple of weeks after Bilbo died. It really hit me one week-end: Bilbo was gone and he wasn't ever coming back. I had been doing all right those first two weeks, but when it hit me, it *really* hit me.

After work one day, on my way home I cracked and stopped at the store and stocked up with a week's worth of alcohol – six bottles of wine. Then I shut myself inside Chez Choo Choo and drank the lot. I was a total mess. I was ranting and raving and effing and blinding as all the pent-up grief came out. Looking out of the window I could see Leroy working in his garden and he could obviously hear me carrying on because he came over to see me and gave me a hug. I was paralytic and emotional. 'I really love you, mate,' I slurred. Even in my inebriated state I could see that Leroy was shocked to see me like that. In fact he later admitted that he had been worried for my safety that day. 'In my heart of hearts I thought you were going to do something silly,' he said. But he said that all the while he could lean out of his kitchen window and hear music, amongst the swearing, he knew I was all right.

Others too had seen it coming because I had, they said, 'been too calm'. Some of my friends had lost partners and knew a thing or two about the different stages of grief. They knew that the anger had to come out at some point. Some commented afterwards that they had been waiting for it to happen. 'You needed to get that bit over with, Steve,' they said.

Of course it wasn't only Bilbo I was grieving for. I was still getting over the death of my mum and the trauma of having to clear her house. Not to mention walking away from my homeland, not knowing how or when I would return. I missed the old days. Bilbo had been such a big part of who I was for so long, and now that he had gone I felt in danger of disappearing myself. My friends and family were worried about me but I was incapable of doing anything about it. The previous five years had just been awful and I was full of sadness and bitterness and, yes, self-pity too.

Even now, quite often I'll be sitting here thinking: Is this it? What happens now? Because my life has completely changed. Lifeguarding has been my life and it has been hard to adjust to not doing it anymore. I had the perfect life. I had a room with a view and my office was a beach. I was king of my own empire. It had all taken a terrible toll on me, losing my mum and changing jobs. As Leroy put it so eloquently: 'It was like someone had flipped the bus upside down.' He said it was horrible to see, and it was certainly horrible to experience.

After Bilbo passed away I spent a lot of time thinking back to the good old days when we worked on the beach together. Leroy is one of my best mates and sometimes he used to walk down to the beach at about half past six to meet me for a drink after work. We'd be gasping for a cold beer but it would take us nearly an hour to walk the four hundred metres from the lifeguard hut to the Old Success Inn because we would be stopped by kids every few metres wanting to meet Bilbo. And I would never say no to them.

Of course I have my family. They still live in Penzance and are all successful in their own right. I'm really proud of all of my children and the thing I'm really pleased about is that I've never met anybody who has a bad word to say about any of them. As I write, Charlie has been a firefighter since leaving the Royal Marines. He is married to Shelley, and as well as Holly they have a daughter called Sophia, who is five. Alice, my eldest, works in a restaurant in St Ives, where the customers were always thrilled to hear that she actually knew Bilbo! She and her husband Ben have Ruby and Stan.

And Kate, the youngest of the three, has had her own restaurant in Penzance for a year now. It's called The Front Room and is a quirky establishment, decorated in her own inimitable style. There are vintage suitcases buried in the walls of the tearoom, and a ladies' powder room done out in leopard-print wallpaper with a Barbie doll on the door.

Her boyfriend is Matt Evans, a rugby player for the Cornish Pirates. His career is very much on the up and he played for Canada in the 2015 Rugby World Cup.

Kate's business has been doing really well and in 2015 she was nominated for the *Cornishman* newspaper's Business of the Year Award. It was their annual Community Awards, for people or businesses that had excelled over the year, and Kate was one of the top three nominees for 'outstanding business contribution to the community'. And a certain someone was also in the running for the *Cornishman* awards that year, in the category Teacher of the Year. What's more, he won it!

No, not me – Bilbo! You had to be nominated and apparently lots of people had put Bilbo's name forward. And my boy won it, posthumously. I hadn't been out much since he'd died and had been avoiding people. But when I was invited to the awards ceremony I knew it was something I had to do. More than that, I *wanted* to do it because I knew it would be in the local press and would be a wonderful tribute to Bilbo. I thought that anything that presented him in a good light was worth doing. I didn't know that he was going to win it, obviously, but I did write a little speech just in case. It was hard writing it because it was still so raw, but I just focused on what I had to do.

The ceremony was to be held at the Carbis Bay Hotel near St Ives, at the beginning of September 2015. But because all my clothes had been sponsored and I hadn't bought anything for years, I didn't even own a suit. I asked an old friend of mine if I could borrow something, because he's got quite a dapper wardrobe. He's about the same size as me and I thought he might have a lounge suit I could wear. He said, 'Yes, as a matter of fact I've got just the thing but it's quite a good suit, so for God's sake don't get plastered and drop wine all over it, J'mo!'

I said, 'I'm not going to be drinking, so don't worry about that.' I had to have a good spruce-up because it was one of those evenings where all the local dignitaries were out in their evening dress. There was an old lady in her eighties who had been collecting for a charity for years and she got up before her name was even read out because she was determined that she was going to win Volunteer of the Year! There was also a little girl who had raised fifty-two thousand pounds for a local children's hospice by playing the violin.

We sat down at the table and after our orders had been taken the wine waiter turned up and asked people what they would like to drink. He went off and as he came back through the door I thought: He doesn't look like a wine waiter to me – he's not very steady on his feet. He was a bit like the waiter in the Peter Sellers film *The Party*! He had this tray with a bottle of red wine, a glass of orange juice and a glass of white wine, and as he reached over to place the bottle on the table, the orange juice and glass of white wine just went all over me.

Or, more to the point, all over my lovely (borrowed!) grey linen suit. I couldn't believe it. But thank goodness it wasn't the red. Someone rushed over and asked if I wanted them to wash the jacket but I said, 'No, no, please just take it away and dry it.' Because if Bilbo *was* to win, I would have to go and stand on the podium under the lights to accept the award and make the speech.

The reckoning was spot-on as it turned out. Not only

that, I subsequently found out that Bilbo had received more nominations than all the other nominees put together. The judges said that thousands of people had voted for him. I was so proud. In my speech I said how surprised and honoured I was to be invited to the event, and how sorry that Bilbo couldn't be there to collect the award himself. 'I always knew that Bilbo was unique and that his contribution was valid and important and this award recognizes all of what I believed in,' I said, somehow managing to keep a stiff upper lip for him.

Luckily, there was a happy footnote to the wine-meets-linen-jacket incident too. I managed to have it hand-washed and then took it to the dry cleaners to be pressed and fortunately it didn't stain. Phew!

As a matter of fact, although I didn't tell anyone, Bilbo *had* been at the awards ceremony that night. I'd had him cremated and I carried his remains around with me in a wooden casket inside my rucksack wherever I went, including awards ceremonies! At night he still lies where he always did, now under his portrait. 'Night, Billy,' I say. And in the morning when I head out I swing my rucksack on my back and say, 'Come on, Billy, off we go.'

I even took him with me to London. As I've said, word of Bilbo's passing brought many messages of support and condolence, which were a great comfort to me. And one morning a letter arrived at Chez Choo Choo from an editor at a publishing house, explaining that she knew about Bilbo because her grandmother lives in Penzance. She said she had been sorry to read that he had passed away and was wondering if I would be interested in telling the story of Britain's first lifeguard dog in a book? She said there was absolutely no pressure or obligation for me even to reply, and to just let her know when, and if, I felt ready to consider her proposal.

Well, I didn't know what to think at first. I didn't want anything to do with it to start with. I couldn't even consider it because I was so grief-stricken. I'd just completely crumbled. But then I started to realize that it could be something positive. Something to remind people just how amazing Bilbo was. I must admit that I *have* found the process of writing this book to be painful at times, but I hope that ultimately it will bring me lasting comfort.

I miss the companionship of having a dog, but I don't know yet if I shall get another one. That's the thing about taking on an animal: you know you're going to come up against the pain of losing them again. And as any animal lover will tell you, it is heartbreaking. A friend of mine said that when her three-legged Parson Russell terrier, Chester, died at the grand old age of fourteen and a half, she felt as if her heart had been ripped out, roughly chopped, and stuffed back in. I have to say, I know what she means.

That said, looking back on it all I think the rewards outweigh the emotional loss. I will never forget one time when Bilbo and I were relaxing in the evening sun outside the Old Success Inn with a few friends, Bilbo insisting as usual on *fresh* water. Anyway, there we were, just chilling out, when this chap came over and asked if he could fuss Bilbo. His eyes were full of tears and he said, 'Please, I need my Newfoundland fix!' He went on to explain that he had lost his Newfoundland the year before and was missing him desperately. I have to admit that at the time I didn't quite understand – or appreciate – what he was going on about. But of course I do now.

One day, maybe, I will get another dog. But I will take my time. On the one hand I have thought of going down the re-homing route, and perhaps giving an older dog a few comfortable sunset years. But on the other hand I would quite like a pup to train from day one. Unlike Bilbo, who by the time I adopted him already had a 'handle' on the world around him. I have often wondered how different Bilbo might have been if we had been together from the very start. Not that I'm complaining about the eventual outcome in any way, though.

I have sometimes dog-sat Weetie the Norfolk terrier and he has been to stay at Chez Choo Choo a couple of times. He's actually called Beetroot but everyone calls him Weetie, because who wants to shout '*Beetroot!*' in public? No one, that's who! I was putting him in the car one day when a neighbour walked by and said, 'Have you got a new one?' I explained that I was just looking after him, and he nodded sagely and said, 'He ain't nothing like the King, is he?'

It *was* different with Bilbo because he was a working dog. He had a purpose in life, which kept him happy. He definitely wasn't just a pet. But I would love another Newfoundland, I'll admit. I'd want a brown one like Bilbo, though, if only for the reduced slobber factor! Bilbo enjoyed visiting my friends with me. Initially, most would be very welcoming but for some the novelty soon wore off. Going anywhere with Bilbo was a bit like travelling with Sir Elton John or Dame Joan Collins – he always came with a lot of luggage! Towels, flannels, grooming kit, water bowl, large flagon of water, just in case, and, of course, food.

Water was the most important factor and when we arrived anywhere, out would come the water bowl and the inevitable moat of water around it after Bilbo had had a thirsty drink. Suffice to say, you really needed to be a dog lover to want him in your home! Be that as it may, there were those who did not object to Bilbo in the slightest. I remember being at a party in Newlyn one autumn night. It had been a late one and Bilbo and I had been put up in the spare room. Bilbo, although initially wanting to be with me, would wait until I was sound asleep and then go exploring, creeping stealthily around the house on his big cushioned pads. This particular night, it was quite warm and he had managed to climb into the tiled Jacuzzi to sleep. During a night-time visit to the toilet, my friend was suddenly aware of a heavy breathing behind him. Slowly turning round, his heart in his mouth, he saw nothing, hearing only the unmistakable sound of snoring coming from the Jacuzzi. Peering over the edge, he spied Bilbo, one eye open now that his snooze had been disturbed. Breathing a sigh of relief, my friend simply backed away and returned to bed. He said he had completely forgotten that we were staying the night.

About two months after Bilbo died, Leroy came to see me. Over the years he often popped by with a few beers after he'd put his baby to bed and the two of us would play some dominoes and chew the fat. Oft-times his black and white cat, Tubbs, would follow him and we'd hear her scratching. On moving the curtain aside, we would see a black nose and two white paws clinging to the window frame. He'd open the door for her and she'd swing in.

And then she'd see Bilbo and you could see her think-ing: It's a dog! Tubbs ordinarily couldn't stand dogs, and if she saw one her hair would stand on end and she would run a mile. But with Bilbo it was a different story. He would just raise his big head and let out a groan and go back to sleep and the cat would relax. Sometimes Tubbs would come and sit and look at Bilbo even when Leroy wasn't around, although she was always a bit apprehensive because he was so big. They never played together but I always got the impression that the cat wanted to, because of the way she came to seek him out.

On this particular evening, Tubbs had followed Leroy up to my cabin and was peering in the door and looking round as if to say, 'Well, where is he?' She came inside and was creeping around, looking in every nook and cranny. And then she went over to my rucksack, where the casket with Bilbo's ashes was, and the next minute she had climbed into the bag and was purring and rubbing herself all over it.

Now, how on earth did the cat know what was in that bag? She had never showed the slightest interest in my rucksack before, so I think she must have sensed Bilbo's presence in the room – just as I still do. It was really poign-ant, and made me realize that Bilbo had touched the lives of many creatures, not just human ones.

Epilogue

After Bilbo passed away Linda bought a miniature weeping willow which I planted on her land by the place in the stream where he used to love to lie, cooling off while watching the dragonflies and mayflies flitting everywhere. It is a comfort to see it growing and thriving.

And Mark, who is now head of Ceramics at Falmouth Art College, has come up with the wonderful idea of commissioning a statue of Bilbo. He said his students could make a life-sized – or even larger – sculpture as a project, and we would just have to pay for the materials and for a professional sculptor to put his face on at the end. He thinks it would cost something in the region of four to five thousand pounds, as opposed to the thirty thousand pounds we would need for a specialist sculptor to undertake the project. I have a huge black bin bag full of Bilbo's fur that I plan to make a blanket out of one day. It needs to be spun into wool with lambs' wool – it's called chiengora.

The Jubilee Lido in Penzance, which is a spectacular art deco outdoor pool, is being refurbished and is due to open in the summer of 2016. I think it would be great to have a statue of Bilbo on the promenade near there, looking out to sea for all time. He would also be looking out over the finish line of the Newlyn to Penzance annual swim. Of course we would need permission from the council, not to mention raising the money to pay for it, but it is early days and it is nice to have something to focus on.

In November 2015, six months after Billy died, I went for a five-mile speed walk and took him with me in my rucksack. Maybe I shouldn't have because even as ashes he is quite heavy and I was probably carrying about forty pounds on my back. Climbing back up the cliff, I was relieved to be back home as I wouldn't have wanted to do an extra mile – let's put it that way! I decided then that he could stay home next time. After all, it was too much for him in real life anyway.

The amount of love I had for Bilbo and the devastation I felt when he died was something I could barely cope with at times, to be honest. But it's over and I'm through it, and for the first time since Bilbo died I find myself looking forward instead of backwards.